REVITALISING LAGGING REGIONS

SMART SPECIALISATION AND INDUSTRY 4.0

MARIACHIARA BARZOTTO, CARLO CORRADINI, FELICIA M FAI,
SANDRINE LABORY AND PHILIP R TOMLINSON

RSA Regional Studies Association

A leading & impactful community

First published 2019
by Taylor & Francis
4 Park Square, Milton Park, Abingdon, Oxon, OX14 4RN

Taylor & Francis Group, an informa business

British Library Cataloguing-in-Publication Data
A catalogue record for this book is available from the British Library.

ISBN13: 978-0-367-42271-4 (print)
ISBN13: 978-0-367-42274-5 (e-book)

Typeset in 10.5/13.5 Univers LT Std
by Nova Techset Private Limited, Bengaluru and Chennai, India

CONTENTS

REVITALISING LAGGING REGIONS: SMART SPECIALISATION AND INDUSTRY 4.0

FOREWORD

Smart specialisation has been increasingly acknowledged in the scientific community and among policy-makers as a distinctive made-in-EU initiative with regard to place-based innovation strategies. Although it is a relatively young concept, its application has been hugely supported in the context of EU regional policy through both ex-ante conditionality provisions and remarkable budgetary allocations, as well as the deployment of a number of supporting tools and initiatives. The uptake of smart specialisation has progressively gained momentum beyond the mere legal requirements, although such uptake has not been homogeneous across EU countries and regions.

Any consideration about the performance of smart specialisation so far cannot ignore the specific case of lagging regions. Not only is this a key issue (and allocation priority) for EU regional policy, and therefore a key element of success or failure, it may also represent a crucial turning point for the application and acceptance of smart specialisation in broader contexts. This comes at a moment in time when smart specialisation is becoming of interest to countries across the world, who also face tough transitions and challenges that go beyond the traditional innovation domain and incorporate societal and sustainability elements. For instance, smart specialisation in EU lagging regions is gradually taken as a reference framework for applications in EU enlargement and neighbourhood countries, where the issue of institutional capacity is even more urgent and also embraces questions related to the openness and democratisation of policy processes.

Applying smart specialisation in lagging regions is not only about setting priorities for local innovation policies or supporting continuous stakeholder involvement, but indeed it is about creating and nurturing regional innovation ecosystems that work and innovation communities that have a say in shaping the destiny of the place they live and operate in. This means taking a broader view of innovation, beyond the technological elements, enhancing the role of institutions and local coalitions of actors, and building both capacities and trust.

This Regional Studies Policy Expo book comes at the right moment in time, when preparation of the post-2020 EU policy cycle is intensively developing and both taking stock and reflection on the experience gained so far. This book can timely feed into the ongoing discussions at European Commission level, on which smart specialisation 2.0 will be shaped.

https://doi.org/10.1080/2578711X.2019.1621090

The book's contribution sheds light on the crucial challenge of making lagging regions fully own and benefit from smart specialisation, while digitisation and industry 4.0 show that important changes in economic, social and technological systems are about to come. This might be perceived as a threat for lagging regions, in consideration of their vulnerability and the weakness of their innovation ecosystems, but at the same time it can offer encouraging perspectives and suggest appropriate trajectories in order to turn this challenge into an opportunity for a brighter future.

Alessandro Rainoldi
Head of Unit, Territorial Development European Commission,
Joint Research Centre Seville, Spain
Alessandro.Rainoldi@ec.europa.eu

FOREWORD

Following the first formulation of the smart specialisation strategies concept (S3) in 2009, the integration of this approach into EU innovation policies has been rapid and the *ex-ante* conditionality mechanism has led to a massive implementation of S3 in European regions through EU cohesion policy.

Even though the rapidity of the transition from idea to practice may have seemed excessive, it also resulted in a positive mobilisation and commitment of the regions as well as an accelerated collective learning process regarding S3 procedures and practices, thanks especially to the very intense interactions between the academic community, policymakers at regional level and the different expertise units set up by the European Commission (particularly the JRC S3 platform). Another characteristic of this accelerated learning process has been the commitment on the part of the regions to learn for themselves by analysing and comparing their experiences in a very decentralised and spontaneous way.

Today, on the eve of the next programming period, we can confirm that the raison d'être of this approach as well as its basic principles still remain valid and what's more we're better at "doing" an S3 today than we were a few years ago. These are all important lessons for the next version of the cohesion policy programme under discussion and preparation in Brussels and the European capitals for 2021.

Raison d'être and basic principles still valid!

The S3 approach focuses on the deployment of innovative activity within the region, enabling the region concerned to change and develop new competitive advantages based upon these transformations. The other raison d'être of S3 is to encourage regions to build these competitive advantages on their specific strengths, potentials and opportunities, rather than imitating what other regions do; in other words, the same "good" things, which in the end will in many cases prove inconsistent and unrelated to the region's existing assets and potentials.

To attain these very general objectives, the principles identified in 2009 remain valid:

https://doi.org/10.1080/2578711X.2019.1621092

- *Concentrate on establishing certain priorities.* This principle aims to generate a certain density of actors and projects that are *related* as they are dedicated to the same priority – an imperative condition to benefit from the resulting synergies, complementarity and agglomeration, which are essential determinants of innovation, creativity and R&D productivity.
- *Concentrate not on structures (for example the region's three most important industries) but on the transformation of these structures.* Each priority includes one or several sectors and a direction of change – a direction sufficiently well-defined to create the density effects mentioned above.
- *Favour a logic of entrepreneurial discovery,* which means simply that the targeted transformation will follow a path that is not decided from the top but will be discovered as the process unfolds. There is therefore no *ex ante* plan, which implies rigorous feedback, monitoring and flexibility mechanisms.

The S3 approach is thus marked by both a high level of intentionality and prioritisation – the region regains control of its destiny – and a high level of discovery and initiative by the actors of the innovation process. It is this combination of two policy logics – frequently opposed in the literature and in practice – that constitute its trade-mark! As so well expressed by Paul David – one of the concept's three authors – S3 is neither totally 'top down' nor purely 'bottom up': *"The S3 approach is about designing an intermediate process aiming to enhance entrepreneurial efforts and coordination within a framework (a strategic priority) structured by the government."*[1]

We are better at "doing" an S3 nowadays

Thanks to the massive exercise of implementation since 2012 and the first lessons learned from it, we are now able to identify certain conditions or provisions that at the time seemed absolutely vital for the success of the approach but that henceforth seem less necessary or even useless and harmful. We can consequently propose a more simple and obvious process - a process that regions will find it easier to implement – while its effectiveness will no doubt be greater.

In particular it has become obvious that an S3 must not rely on an immutable formula that everyone must adhere to in order to avoid failure – like the 10 Commandments! Let's leave regions the freedom to invent their own approach, while still insisting on the necessity of adhering to a few generic principles and processes in order to identify priorities, translate each priority into a transformational roadmap and design an action plan to support the development of the corresponding transformative activity. Here we can be inspired by the idea of a script: a set of simple rules like those the theatrical director gives the actor he is asking to improvise concerning a certain theme.

The unique experience of S3 over the past few years has led to an enormous learning process regarding conditions and procedures of implementation. Thanks to an impressive collective effort between academic researchers and policymakers – accompanied by the European Commission – surprising progress has been made. This progress has concerned the academic aspect; thus the domain of innovation policy research has changed considerably within a few years (particularly thanks to the work on S3). But it has concerned especially the practical aspect as now we have achieved an implementation concept, which is consistent with the theory, is ambitious and whose feasibility has been proved.[2] The collection of chapters offered in this RSA Expo book and is focussed on a specific S3 domain (the revitalisation of lagging regions) reflects the progress on both the academic side and the practical side of policy design and implementation. It is a welcome addition.

Dominique Foray

Chair of Economics and Management of Innovation –

College of Management – Ecole Polytechnique Fédérale de Lausanne, Switzerland

dominique.foray@epfl.ch

REFERENCES

1 David P (2019) Personal communication.

2 Berkowitz P, Foray D, Eichler M and Przeor M (forthcoming) *Milestones on the Road to the Next S3 Period*, working paper, DG Regio.

CONTRIBUTORS

ABOUT THE EDITORS

Mariachiara Barzotto is an Assistant Professor in International Business at Newcastle University, UK

Carlo Corradini is an Associate Professor in Regional Economics in the Department of Management at the University of Birmingham, UK

Felicia M Fai is an Associate Professor in International Business in the School of Management at the University of Bath, UK

Sandrine Labory is an Associate Professor in the Department of Economics at the University of Ferrara, Italy

Philip R Tomlinson is an Associate Professor in Business Economics in the School of Management at the University of Bath, UK

OTHER CONTRIBUTORS

David Bailey is Professor of Industrial Strategy in the Department of Management at the University of Birmingham, UK

Lisa De Propris is Professor of Regional Economic Development in the Department of Management at the University of Birmingham, UK

Kevin Morgan is Professor of Governance and Development in the School of Geography and Planning at the University of Cardiff, UK.

Philip McCann is Professor in Urban and Regional Economics at University of Sheffield Management School, UK

https://doi.org/10.1080/2578711X.2019.1621094

Raquel Ortega-Argilés is Professor in Regional Economic Development in the Department of Strategy and International Business and the City-REDI Institute at the University of Birmingham, UK

Jonathan Potter is Head of Entrepreneurship Policy and Analysis Unit, Centre for Entrepreneurship, SMEs, Regions and Cities at the Organisation for Economic Co-operation and Development (OECD) and a Visiting Professor in the Department of Management at Birkbeck, University of London, UK

Helen Lawton Smith is Professor of Entrepreneurship in the Department of Management at Birkbeck, University of London, UK

Sonja Šlander is a Lecturer in the Faculty of Economics, University of Ljubljana, Slovenia.

Peter Wostner is Head of the Smart Specialisation Unit, at the Government Office for Development and European Cohesion Policy, Republic of Slovenia.

EXECUTIVE SUMMARY

This *Regional Studies* Policy Expo book brings together leading experts to explore how lagging regions can develop and benefit from an appropriate Smart Specialisation Strategy (S3) and also take advantage of the opportunities of digitalisation and Industry 4.0 (I4.0). While S3 has quickly become the major component of the European Union's (EU) Innovation policy through its Research and Innovation Strategies for Smart Specialisation (RIS3) programme, its ability to revitalise lagging regions has so far been relatively limited.

To a large extent, this reflects the significant challenges faced by lagging regions in participating in the RIS3 programme. The underlying logic of S3 is to prioritise the use of public funds to support actions and/or 'activities' in particular technological fields (at the regional level) which have the potential for innovation, 'entrepreneurial discovery' and commercial gain. Such opportunities tend to reside in more dynamic regions, which are blessed with greater entrepreneurial and technological capabilities and good networks for knowledge exchange. In contrast, in lagging regions the prevalence of low tech sectors, an over dependence upon traditional and/or declining industries, weak business and knowledge networks and a lack of institutional capacity make it difficult to identify new 'activities' or 'market opportunities' for policy support. As such, S3 may actually exacerbate regional imbalances and run counter to current EU cohesion policy. The emergence of new technologies associated with I4.0 also tends to favour more dynamic regions, and is likely to deepen regional divides.

This book makes the case for a better understanding of both S3 and I4.0 and the challenges that lagging regions face in participating in RIS3. It explores how lagging regions can address their inherent weaknesses, and benefit from extra-regional collaboration, skills and technological upgrading and hence take advantage of both S3 and I4.0. In doing so, the book draws upon case evidence from across Europe to highlight how lagging regions are seeking to embrace and implement both S3 and I4.0, and examines how policy might be tailored to enable them to pursue a new innovation-led pathway. This is especially timely, given the EU is about to embark upon Horizon Europe, its 2021–2027 €100 billion research and innovation programme.

https://doi.org/10.1080/2578711X.2019.1621095

KEY RECOMMENDATIONS

1. BUILDING UPON PLACE-SPECIFIC ASSETS

Both 'related technological diversification'/diversification through 'related variety' and 'entrepreneurial discovery' lie at the core of S3, and offer the best opportunity for lagging regions to revitalise their economies within the RIS3 framework.

Policy prioritisation needs to be focused and future-oriented, targeting resources on those activities, technologies or sectors where a region has the most realistic chance to develop. There is significant evidence that regions prosper by diversifying and branching into new technologies, activities and skills-sets by building upon their existing place-specific capabilities and knowledge base, albeit combining them in new ways, to novel applications. In this regard, a regionally-based skills programme, geared towards existing sectoral strengths, but which also encompasses a broader skill-set for promising and/or emerging sectors is particularly relevant.

Policy-makers need to explicitly recognise this point, rather than attempting to replicate and apply policies that may have worked in quite different places. This is especially important where public resources are being used to attract inward investment into regions and/or in seeking to capitalize on the opportunities of I4.0.

2. ENHANCING THE REGIONAL INNOVATION ECO-SYSTEM (RIE)

The success of S3 depends upon effective local knowledge exchange and dissemination processes. Critical to this is a well-functioning Regional Innovation Eco-system (RIE).

In lagging regions, policy should aim to enhance the RIE through building and strengthening local institutions and networks across government, business, public research centres and higher education institutes (HEIs). Doing so will build social and cultural capital and support mutually reinforcing investments and collaborative actions. Policy should also seek to support and exploit the presence of leading HEIs and large firms as regional anchors, as important sponsors of innovation and entrepreneurship within the RIE. This can stimulate innovation dynamics and the 'entrepreneurial discovery' process.

3. STRENGTHENING EXTRA-REGIONAL COLLABORATION

For lagging regions, extra-regional collaboration can be especially beneficial if it facilitates earlier adoption of new I4.0 technologies, knowledge exchange and enhanced capabilities that open up new entrepreneurial opportunities.

RIS3 and EU programmes such as INTERREG play a critical facilitating role in nurturing a broad range of extra-regional collaborations. These initiatives connect actors from disparate regions and offer the potential to enhance science and innovation, while concomitantly fostering better cohesion. Participation also raises a lagging region's international profile and improves policy learning at both administrative and industry levels. This is important for both the successful design and implementation of S3.

However, existing policy frameworks tend to adopt a 'one-size fit all' approach to S3 and RIS3, often ignoring the differences between lagging and advanced regions, and the different incentives required to participate in extra-regional collaboration. Policy needs to be more flexible to account for such differences and enable EU extra-regional collaborative frameworks to be tailored more closely to specific regional RIS3 objectives.

4. TECHNOLOGICAL UPGRADING AND I4.0

Future prosperity will also depend upon identifying, nurturing and diffusing the key I4.0 cross-cutting technologies (e.g. digitalisation, the internet of things, robotics and artificial intelligence) that have an enabling role across both manufacturing and services. In this regard, there is significant scope for EU innovation programmes to recognise and exploit such technologies by making them accessible to businesses in different regions

Such technologies have the potential to transform the potential of lagging regions. Policy can facilitate crossovers between manufacturing (and service) industries and between manufacturing and new technologies. This could come via knowledge transfer mechanisms that connect firms from related and unrelated sectors such as staff exchanges, entrepreneurship programmes, enhanced inter-sectoral labour mobility and research collaboration.

5. EMBRACING SOCIAL INNOVATION AND THE FOUNDATIONAL ECONOMY.

For many lagging regions, the main base of economic activity is the Foundational Economy (FE), which encompasses the essential goods and services of everyday life. Consequently, there is a tendency for citizens in lagging regions to feel excluded from RIS3 initiatives that tend to focus upon a narrow band of advanced technology sectors in pursuit of economic competitiveness.

The next wave of EU funding (2021–2027) offers a great opportunity for EU Innovation frameworks to be more proactive in promoting social innovation (in fields such as renewable energy, healthy ageing, education and food) and developing the FE at the regional level. This will steer innovation policy onto 'issues that matter' at the local level.

Such a policy transformation will require strong political will and a break from conventional top–down policy initiated by central governments. It will also involve a redrawing of economic and social policy objectives, particularly at a local level. This will require greater community led involvement through coalitions of regional and local actors, and an acceptance that policy will entail learning from experiments and social innovation.

Mariachiara Barzotto
mariachiara.barzotto@newcastle.ac.uk

Carlo Corradini
c.corradini@bham.ac.uk

Felicia M Fai
mnsfmf@bath.ac.uk

Sandrine Labory
sandrine.labory@unife.it

Philip R Tomlinson
mnsprt@bath.ac.uk

1. INTRODUCTION

Smart Specialisation (S3) has quickly become the major component of the European Union's (EU) Innovation policy through the Research and Innovation Strategies for Smart Specialisation (RIS3) programme. The basic premise of S3 is a public-private partnership in which public funds are prioritised to support 'activities' in particular technological fields at the regional level which have the potential for innovation, 'entrepreneurial discovery' and commercial gain. RIS3 seeks to achieve this through a 'bottom–up process' involving local stakeholders and which deliberately builds upon a region's existing and historic advantages and capabilities. It is anticipated these may be combined with new general purpose technologies (GPTs) such as ICT, electronics, and digitalisation which are driving the emergence of Industry 4.0 (I4.0) so as to stimulate knowledge and innovation opportunities. As such, S3 has been labelled as being 'place-based' and is a return to a more selective (and vertical) mode of industrial policy intervention.

There has been much rhetorical excitement surrounding RIS3, especially in its perceived potential to generate an industrial renaissance in mature industrial and lagging regions by breathing life into new 'phoenix' industries. Yet the inherent logic of S3 can extenuate regional imbalances since it may unduly favour more dynamic and leading regions, where greater entrepreneurial and technological capabilities and good networks already reside, and from which new opportunities are more likely to arise. Indeed, much of the empirical evaluation of RIS3 has so far tended to focus upon its application in more dynamic and exemplar regional contexts. In contrast, in lagging regions with 'hollowed out' manufacturing bases these capabilities are significantly diminished, which weakens their ability to participate in and benefit from RIS3 initiatives.

S3 was, in part, an EU response to the Great Financial Crisis to ignite European innovation and productivity growth at the regional level, and in this context has been described as the biggest and boldest experiment in regional industrial policy ever implemented.[1] Yet the capacity of S3 to transform the growth potential of lagging regions has been seriously questioned. Indeed, since 2008 there has been a significant reversal of the trend towards widespread inter-regional convergence to one of widening inter-regional divergence in terms of economic performance.[2] This consequently represents a significant challenge to the legitimacy of RIS3, especially given the difficulties of reconciling the possible adverse impacts of the implementation of S3 for balanced regional growth within the context of the EU's wider policy aims of building *'inclusive, innovative and reflective societies*[3] and EU 2014–2020 Cohesion policy.

These issues are especially pertinent with the challenges and opportunities associated with Industry 4.0 (I4.0) and the so-called Fourth Industrial Revolution. This refers to increasing automation, digitalisation and data exchange in manufacturing technologies such as artificial intelligence, robotics, cyber-physical systems, the Internet of things and cloud computing. The emergence of these new technologies will cause major disruption to processes in both manufacturing and services. For example, digitalisation will open up new opportunities for the interaction between producers and consumers, possibly enabling the creation of entirely new businesses or transforming existing ones through the creation of new platforms and big data analytics. This can offer lagging regions the

https://doi.org/10.1080/2578711X.2019.1621096

potential to re-invigorate traditional industries through greater product customisation and exploiting new synergies between R&D and manufacturing. In doing so, the re-shoring of production activities may become more attractive.[4]

However, there is a real danger that I4.0 and the uneven distribution of capital intensive manufacturing displacing labour, may unduly favour more dynamic regions and will introduce new layers of socio-economic and regional divides. Indeed, so called digital divides already exist not only between countries, but also between regions in the same country and the rich and poor in society (see Chapter 6). Furthermore, in many lagging regions there is little knowledge and/or adoption of new I4.0 technologies. This makes it extremely difficult for lagging regions to identify the potential and exploit the opportunities of I4.0 in the context of their own industrial base.

Moreover, current policy responses and practices, in the implementation of S3 vary significantly across countries and between regions. The focus tends to be based largely on specific initiatives and projects and a framework characterised by a simple distinction between leading and lagging regions. Where initiatives aimed at lagging regions – such as the RIS3 Lagging Regions project[5] – exist, they have, as yet, tended to offer limited opportunities for a transition towards advanced manufacturing.

This Regional Studies Expo book offers a new set of perspectives on the challenges that lagging regions face when participating in RIS3; how they are seeking to embrace and implement both S3 and I4.0. It specifically explores how lagging regions can address their inherent weaknesses, and benefit from extra-regional collaboration, skills and technological upgrading and hence take advantage of both S3 and I4.0. In doing so, the book draws upon case evidence from lagging regions across Europe, and examines how RIS3 policies might be better tailored to enable them to pursue a new innovation-led pathway. This is especially timely, given the EU will soon commence Horizon Europe, its €100 billion research and innovation programme for 2021–2027.

The book comprises of six further chapters, each written by leading academic and policy experts in S3, I4.0 and place-based industrial strategy. Chapter 2 by Philip McCann and Raquel Ortega-Argilés sets the scene in outlining the basic concepts of S3, before examining the extent to which RIS3 initiatives are employed in lagging regions. In Chapter 3, Mariachiara Barzotto, Carlo Corradini, Felicia Fai, Sandrine Labory and Philip Tomlinson explore the potential benefits and pitfalls for lagging regions from engaging in extra-regional collaboration – especially between lagging and leading regions – using case examples from Cornwall in the UK, and Puglia in Italy. Chapter 4, by Jonathan Potter and Helen Lawton Smith, then considers the Polish experience of implementing S3, focusing on the regions of Pomorskie and Malopolskie. In Chapter 5, Sonja Šlander and Peter Wostner then focus upon the disruptive nature of I4.0 and examine how Slovenia is using S3 and related policies to successfully transition towards the new technologies of I4.0. Chapter 6, by David Bailey and Lisa De Propris considers the potential opportunities and adverse consequences of I4.0, before outlining policy suggestions to ensure lagging regions are able to take advantage. Finally, in Chapter 7, Kevin Morgan draws on the Welsh experience, to make the case for a more inclusive, regionally focused EU innovation policy framework which gives greater weight to social innovation and the Foundational Economy. Each chapter concludes with a set of identified challenges and specific policy recommendations.

Mariachiara Barzotto
mariachiara.barzotto@newcastle.ac.uk

Carlo Corradini
c.corradini@bham.ac.uk

Felicia M Fai
f.m.fai@bath.ac.uk

Sandrine Labory
sandrine.labory@unife.it

Philip R Tomlinson
mnsprt@bath.ac.uk

REFERENCES

1 Radosevic S, Ciampi Stancova K (2018) Internationalising smart specialisation: Assessment and issues in the case of EU new member states. *Journal of the Knowledge Economy*, 9(1): 263–293.

2 European Union (2014) Investment for jobs and growth. Promoting development and good governance in EU Regions and cities: Sixth report on economic, social and territorial cohesion. Brussels: Publications Office of the European Union. Available online at: http://ec.europa.eu/regional_policy/cohesion_report [Accessed 27 February 2019].

3 European Commission (2017) Europe in a changing world – Inclusive, innovative and reflective societies. HORIZON 2020 – Work Programme 2016–2017. Brussels. Available online at: http://ec.europa.eu/research/participants/data/ref/h2020/wp/2016_2017/main/h2020-wp1617-societies_en.pdf [Accessed 27 February 2019].

4 De Propris L and Bailey D (2018) Industry 4.0, new industrial spaces and implications for industrial strategy. In C. Berry (ed.) *What We Really Mean When We Talk About Industrial Strategy*. A Future Economies Publication, Manchester Metropolitan University. https://www2.mmu.ac.uk/media/mmuacuk/content/documents/business-school/future-economies/WHAT_IND-STRAT___BERRY_NOV18.pdf [Accessed 27 February 2019].

5 Further information can be found at: http://s3platform.jrc.ec.europa.eu/ris3-in-lagging-regions [Accessed 27 February 2019].

2. PERSPECTIVES ON SMART SPECIALISATION POLICIES IN LAGGING REGIONS

1. INTRODUCTION

The RIS3 agenda has become a central plank of EU Cohesion policy. It is aimed at spearheading the drive towards research, innovation, and entrepreneurship across all EU regions, especially its weaker and economically lagging regions.[1] In this regard, RIS3 is regarded as a critical component in reversing the widening EU regional imbalances that have arisen since the 2008 global economic crisis.

However, regional innovation ecosystems in lagging regions often appear to be weak. This is largely due to poorly connected industrial and knowledge networks, alongside a lack of technological diversity to take advantage of changing market conditions. These inadequacies are a significant challenge for cohesion policy, which requires enabling lagging regions to find new innovation-led pathways. This will involve the upgrading and diversification of their technological capabilities so they are able to adapt to the modern economic challenges.

This chapter reviews the basic concepts of S3, and how these might be employed to enhance innovation led growth. In doing so, the chapter briefly outlines the extent to which EU smart specialisation initiatives are being adopted in lagging regions.

2. SMART SPECIALISATION STRATEGY (S3): CONCEPT AND BASIC RATIONALE

Many of the building blocks for smart specialisation strategies (S3) were already evident in different forms of modern regional innovation policies. At heart, S3 is a policy prioritisation framework aimed at finding ways to enhance the scale and effectiveness of a region's entrepreneurial and innovation processes.

This is in marked contrast to previous generations of regional development policies. These predominantly focused upon the 'importing' of new technologies (via inward Foreign Direct Investment – FDI). Often, there was a mismatch between new imported technologies and a region's existing technology base,[2] which was also reflected in skills and supply chain mismatches. These misalignments made it difficult to develop technological synergies and new regional growth paths. So, while short-term goals related to employment gains would often be achieved, in the long-run these technology transfer-types of activities were often very limited. Where EU Cohesion Policy resources were employed to facilitate FDI – via for example subsidies for the establishment of special development areas, new infrastructure provision or new land reclamation and rehabilitation activities – the lack of embeddedness and the resulting short lifespans of foreign firms would often act to discredit the policy interventions.

S3 gave rise to a completely new way of thinking about these issues. It focuses upon promoting a region's entrepreneurial and innovation potential. This is best achieved by fostering local entrepreneurial search processes through the ideas, insights and actions of local entrepreneurs which are often the central drivers of change. As such, S3 is about technological and capability upgrading, alongside the diversifying of the regional industrial base. This is especially important in the case of lagging regions since they do not have the capabilities many other regions have. Enhancing capabilities may, however, be achieved through collaborating with external partners – hence the importance of fostering connectivity not only within but critically between regions (see Chapter 3).

https://doi.org/10.1080/2578711X.2019.1621098

It is important to note S3 is not in any way meant to be dirigiste. On the contrary, it is aimed at transforming policy-thinking from traditional top–down and predominantly sectorally-led approaches to a more local, bottom–up innovation-led approach. Such bottom–up approaches may include enhancing local skills and training, accelerating the transfer and adaptation of new technologies, creating incubators and/or cluster policy implementation.[3] However, S3 does not advocate any specific objectives, tools, or programmes. Instead it emphasises the importance of the local policy prioritisation process, where policy interventions to upgrade technological capabilities are identified through local stakeholders. Central to these policy choices is the fostering of local entrepreneurial discovery processes, which involves experimentation and self-discovery.[4]

In a wide variety of contexts, RIS3 policy processes are also being realized via other policies including linking INTERREG projects, Horizon2020 and the Transnational Cooperation and Value-Chains initiative (2016) within RIS3 (see Chapter 3).[5] Since RIS3 includes elements from many other fields, as well as the more traditional elements of regional policy, it means that these other lines of analysis and policy-thinking can also be implemented, harmonised and integrated into national and regional innovation policies.[6]

What is the entrepreneurial discovery process?

This is an interactive process in which entrepreneurs and state funded agencies share information about potential commercial and technological opportunities.

This is part of the prioritisation process to identify new 'activities' for state funding.

Entrepreneurs are ideally placed in markets to identify such opportunities, whereas state agencies can take a longer term view and offer appropriate support to realise them.

Indeed, RIS3 ought to be considered as a policy approach and a process rather than an innovation policy in its own right, and this 'meta role' of RIS3 constitutes both its weakness and its strength. Its weakness is it does not prescribe or implement specific tools for specific actions and, as such, it may have limited ability to reshape and integrate other policy streams. Yet, this meta role is also its strength in that "… *it can help to redefine and reshape other policies by impacting on specific criteria or priorities which these policies need to consider at the regional level*".[7] As such, RIS3 provides an organising framework for marshalling tools and concepts to help regions to identify relevant priorities at the right level of granularity so that implementation of an appropriate action plan becomes realistic and meaningful.

3. POLICY DESIGN, PRIORITISATION AND IMPLEMENTATION

3.1 Design and Prioritisation

To re-emphasise, the key principle of RIS3 is policy resources are prioritised on those activities, technologies or sectors where it is felt a region has the most realistic chance to develop.[8] In terms of the actual policy-prioritisation and policy-design process, S3 has been characterised as being a 'check-and-update' and 'test-and-recast' exercise – it is cognisant of policy limitations and therefore heavily emphasises policy-monitoring and evaluation.[9] From the perspective of EU Cohesion Policy, a major difficulty here is that both the requisite processes of experimentalism and self-discovery as well as the needed checks and updates are especially limited in lagging regions.[10]

In designing a RIS3 approach, many regions have to address a dual problem, namely both the differentiation and the specialisation of their innovation capabilities.[11] On the one hand, differentiation requires regions to explore new combinations of their regional-specific capabilities and regional-specific opportunities. At the same time, specialisation implies regions concentrate their resources, promote agglomeration, encourage related projects and provide new specific public goods in order to promote innovation in a prioritised field.

> **What is technological diversification?**
>
> Expansion of the technology base present in a region into a broader range of technologies.
>
> This technological diversification is most often achieved by combining technologies in related fields (e.g. robotics and automotive) but can also be successful through combining unrelated fields (ICTs and tourism, laser technologies and textiles).

Yet, specialisation and differentiation need not be in conflict with one another, but rather can be mutually aligned within the process of related technological diversification.[12] Recent evidence suggests regional growth is faster and more sustainable in cases where regions diversify and branch into new technologies, activities and skills-sets by building upon their existing capabilities.[13]

This is especially important for lagging regions, which tend to be more reliant for growth via diversification into related technologies, activities, skill-sets and fields. This is because they tend to lack the widespread, and world-class R&D facilities which are required to generate truly radical innovations.[14] For lagging regions, incremental adjustments and adaptation around an existing core and related technologies and capabilities tend to be more meaningful.

Indeed, these types of related diversification processes are far more strategic in nature than the *ad hoc* diversification processes encouraged under previous EU Cohesion Policy, which prioritised the FDI-mediated importation of unrelated technologies, skill-sets and activities. One difficulty is lagging regions often lack the scale economies that can facilitate their positioning in particular market niches. In such cases, it is still sometimes necessary to attract inward investment and/or research teams to catalyse the local processes of change.[15]

Nevertheless, related diversification provides a solid roadmap as to which types of inward investment activities such be targeted. Essentially these should be in those technological areas, which are close, but still somewhat distinct, from a region's existing capabilities. This offers the best opportunity to combine and build synergies in production processes. The case of Italian Slow Food Development is a good example – it promotes linking production, consumption, distribution, and training in the food sector with ethical and 'value-led' behaviour.[16]

3.2 Policy Implementation

The major implementation challenges that smart specialisation strategies typically face are:

(i) RIS3 needs to avoid cases of duplication and imitation where poorly differentiated regions compete for the same resources (and there is no-one EU region that can compete globally);

(ii) RIS3 needs to avoid providing support to isolated and unrelated R&D projects with limited potential to generate local knowledge spill-overs and synergies and limited potential for local longevity;

(iii) RIS3 should be characterised by a higher degree of intentionality and prioritisation compared to generic policies. RIS3 is fundamentally about the logic, design and implementation of a local development strategy, and by necessity, intentionality and prioritisation are the key pillars on which the strategy rests.

Moreover, even with clear policy prioritisation logics and principles, it is still essential that regions aim to find the right granular level – either sectorally, institutionally, technologically or spatially - to put an effective RIS3 programme into operation.[17]

In the context of lagging regions, each of these challenges are to some extent magnified. Dominique Foray (2013)[18] has classified the various technological transition pathways for regional innovation: transition, modernisation, diversification and radical foundation. For lagging regions, the processes of transition, modernisation and diversification seem to be particularly appropriate to facilitate dynamic change, yet in reality these are the most difficult to bring about. In this regard, promoting *extra-regional collaboration* between lagging and leading regions (and nations) may be essential, especially if the latter have complementary knowledge and value-chain configurations. Indeed, fostering such co-operation is now a mainstay of the RIS3 agenda (see Chapter 3).[19]

However, this is not straightforward. Local authorities and business stakeholders in lagging regions are often overly cautious and risk averse, largely due to a lack of experience of successful and widespread change. In addition, entrenched local monopoly/monopsony positions can also block development in lagging regions.[20] These factors promote resistance to RIS3-type changes and, even where ambition and motivation is present, there is often a mismatch between policy ambition and policy capacity. This makes it difficult for lagging regions to exploit the full potential of S3.

Some of these implementation challenges may take on a different order of magnitude over the next few years, as new forms of automation, artificial intelligence and Industry 4.0 take hold (see Chapter 6).[21] At present, it is difficult to identify precisely the outcomes of these technological changes. The current evidence suggests they will have very different impacts in different regions.[22] Given S3 is fundamentally based upon the upgrading of the knowledge-related capabilities within embedded regional activities, RIS3 may play a key role in enhancing the resilience of regions, and their ability to take advantage of newly emerging market possibilities.

4. EVIDENCE FROM THE EU PROGRAMMING PERIOD 2014–2020

RIS3 is beginning to play a major role in stimulating research and innovation-related activities at the regional level in less developed and peripheral EU regions and member states (see Box 1).[23] In addition, a wide range of distinct strategies are being adopted in different places, so the earlier concerns that all regions will end up adopting the same approach have been largely allayed.[24] However, choosing policy priorities and goals for a given region is only a beginning. RIS3 is not intended to be a one-off process, but rather an ongoing process of policy-making and implementation.

Box 1 S3 and EU Funding 2014–2020

In a recent study, Gianelle, Guzzo and Miekowski (2017)[25] analysed 46 Operational Programmes (closed, open and planned calls) in Italy, Poland, Portugal, Czech Republic, Hungary, Lithuania and Slovenia to 31 December 2016. The study found S3 initiatives are being reflected in the increasing share of European Regional Development Funding (ERDF) being allocated to strengthening regional research, technological development, and innovation.

The types of calls examined cover projects involving public funding schemes co-financed by ERDF Thematic Objective 1, alongside resources through national and regional Operational Programmes. Basically, these calls support projects on Research Technological Development and Innovation and they include among them, projects aimed at supporting the creation and strengthening of innovative SMEs via innovation support services, the public procurement of R&D and innovation, innovation prizes, support for research infrastructures, support for business-support organisations, innovation networks and platforms. The level of focus on these types of research and innovation-types of activities is demonstrated, for example, in the case of Poland, whereby some 46.1% of S3-related calls come under Thematic Objective 1 covering an overall ERDF funding of €8.3 billion.

Across different EU regions and member states the types of activities coming under RIS3 proposals varies enormously. As well as stimulating R&D and ICT-adoption, these also include measures promoting technology absorption, enhancing managerial capabilities, skills upgrading and lifelong learning, along with projects involving graduate attraction and absorption. These measures involve activities related to the technological upgrading of SMEs, and also projects involving collaboration with research centres via the use of knowledge vouchers and technical training.

At a higher level, these interventions are all aimed at increasing local business competitiveness, by supporting business growth, cluster formation, and especially by promoting internationalisation and export propensity. However, these policy priorities and interventions are not only focused on high-tech sectors but also on lower-tech and more traditional sectors such as agri-food, forestry, tourism, and textiles. In these established sectors, the aim is to facilitate more incremental innovation across a large base which will allow the sectors to evolve in a more dynamic manner over time, and especially to develop a stronger place-based regional innovation eco-system.

Part of these transition and evolutionary processes may involve promoting connections between industrial and knowledge-generation actors, aimed at addressing mismatches through a 'Triple-Helix' type of framework. Importantly, the identification of potential local strengths and market opportunities which can be developed via the entrepreneurial discovery processes is crucial, as boosting R&D alone is not necessarily a solution. Indeed, boosting R&D alone may exacerbate what is sometimes known as the '*European Paradox*', whereby strong R&D outputs exist alongside weak R&D demand that does not match local needs.[26] RIS3 was designed to specifically avoid such circumstances, with the focus here being on the link between research and innovation and the wider processes of knowledge diffusion and dissemination.

One of the current priority programmes of the RIS3 Platform, concerns the challenge of establishing and driving smart specialisation in low growth and low-income regions (see Box 2). By documenting and sharing the experiences of participating regions, this programme aims to develop policy-making guidance which can be disseminated more widely along with a policy-making 'tool-box' for other EU regions, as well as contributing to advancing to the theoretical principles regarding the implementation of smart specialisation.[27] The regions participating in the programme are classified into low-growth and low-income regions. The low-growth regions are: Puglia from Italy, Centro from Portugal, Extremadura from Spain and all of the Greek regions; while the low-income regions participating in the programme are: Severen Tsentralen from Bulgaria, Észak-Alföld in Hungary, Warminsko Masurskie in Poland, and Nord-Est and Nord-Vest in Romania.

Box 2 EU Initiatives in Lagging Regions

The European Commission has made serious efforts to assist EU regions in their priority-setting and policy-making activities, and this role is spearheaded by the RIS3 Platform based at the EU Joint Research Centre at Seville. The RIS3 platform combines research with the policy-making experience of numerous different regions, allowing regions to share experiences, best-practice and to foster mutual learning processes. For example, the European Commission has also set up what are known as '*Smart Specialisation Thematic Platforms*', which are instruments to support bottom-up collaboration between businesses and researchers along value chains across the EU. The goals of the three S3 Thematic Platforms[28] are to:

- Promote complementarity of regional funding for innovation in specific smart specialisation areas (Key Enabling Technologies, service innovation or resource efficiency).
- Target key political priorities in order to facilitate the emergence of transnational projects to modernise EU industry.
- Boost Europe's competitiveness by moving into commercialisation and scale-up phases.

By December 2018, a total of 28 existing thematic partnerships supported by the three S3 Thematic Platforms were already in place with more than 100 EU regions participating across a wide range of different sectors and approaches.

5. CHALLENGES AND POLICY RECOMMENDATIONS

Challenge 1

RIS3 is beginning to play a major role in how regions are developing their policy-settings, especially in lagging regions. Yet, identifying S3 goals for a given region is only a beginning. RIS3 is not a one-off process, but rather an on-going process of policy learning, experimentation and implementation.

Critical to this process is education and learning about S3, especially among policy-makers in lagging regions, which have less experience of these type of initiatives and lack the institutional capacity to undertake them. Many regional policy-makers are unaware of the concepts behind RIS3 and 'smart specialisation' is often a ubiquitous term to access EU funding programmes.

Policy initiatives such as the Stairway to Excellence Pilot Project[29] may offer opportunities to address these problems.

Challenge 2

The benefits of RIS3 are multi-dimensional rather than being purely technological and commercial, as they also heavily involve institutional and governance issues, including engagement and participation between public, private and civil society stakeholders.

This is especially challenging in lagging regions – particularly in Central and Eastern Europe – since they traditionally display the weakest and least robust governance arrangements. In these cases, RIS3 poses serious challenges and demands on fragile or limited institutional frameworks.

Policy Recommendation 1

The success of S3 depends upon effective local knowledge-dissemination processes. These must involve both manufacturing and services and be set in the context of the upgrading of product and technology value-chains.[30]

In many cases, this will mean reconfiguring value-chains – especially where this involves the opening up and connecting of local business networks to macro-regional and European-wide knowledge networks. In these situations, there is a challenge to develop synergies and complementarities between local business actors and wider networks (see Chapter 3). In some cases, this may be rather threatening to those local actors who are in already-established monopoly positions. This may generate some resistance to change.

Various initiatives have begun to assist regions in adapting to changes, such as the Vanguard Initiative[31] various transnational and cross-border cooperation projects, as well as projects undertaken via INTERREG programmes. Going forward such initiatives will need to be strengthened.

Policy Recommendation 2

Related technological diversification and entrepreneurial discovery lie at the core of S3, and offer the best opportunity for lagging regions to revitalise their economies within the RIS3 framework.

Policy needs to explicitly recognise this, especially where public resources are being utilised in attracting inward investment into regions and/or for supporting extra-regional collaboration (see Chapter 3).

Philip McCann
p.mccann@sheffield.ac.uk

Raquel Ortega-Argilés
R.OrtegaArgiles@bham.ac.uk

REFERENCES

1 McCann P and Ortega-Argilés R (2016) The early experience of smart specialisation implementation in EU cohesion policy. *European Planning Studies*, 24(8):1407–1427.
Foray D, Morgan K and Radosevic S (2017) The role of smart specialisation in the EU research and innovation policy landscape. European Commission. Available online at: https://ec.europa.eu/regional_policy/sources/docgener/brochure/smart/role_smartspecialisation_ri.pdf [Accessed 27 February 2019].
Gianelle C, Kyriakou D, Cohen C and Przeor M (2016) *Implementing smart specialisation: A handbook*. EUR 28053 EN, Brussels: European Commission.

2 Bedreaga IR, Ortega-Argilés R and McCann P. (2018) Multinational performance and the geography of FDI: Issues of embeddeness, strategic fit and the dimensions of distance. In J Beaverstock (ed.) *The Routledge Companion to the Geography of International Business*. London: Routledge.

3 Nauwelaers C, Perianez-Forte I and Midtkandal I (2014) RIS3 implementation and policy mixes. S3 Policy Brief Series,No. 07/2014, JRC Technical Reports Series. European Commission-Joint Research Centre. Luxembourg: Publications Office of the European Union.

4 Foray D, Goddard J, Goenaga XG, Landabaso M, McCann P, Morgan K, Nauwelaers C, Ortega-Argiles R and Mulatero F (2012) *Guide to research and innovation strategies for smart specialisation (RIS3)*. European Commission-Joint Research Centre. Luxembourg: Publications Office of the European Union.

5 Cortijo MA, Esparza RM, Fernández TS, Marinelli E and Arregui EP (2018) *Synergies between Interreg Europe and Smart Specialisation: A Methodological Proposal to Enhance Policy Learning*. JRC Technical Papers, EUR 29390 EN. Luxembourg: Publications Office of the European Union, ISBN 978-92-79-96382-7, doi:10.2760/572859, JRC113414.
Mariussen Å, Rakhmatullin R and Stanionyte L (2016) Smart specialisation: Creating growth through trans-national cooperation and value chains. JRC Science for Policy Report, EUR 28049 EN. Luxembourg: Publications Office of the European Union, doi:10.2791/658931.
Pontikakis D, Doussineau M, Harrap N and Boden M (2018) Mobilising European Structural and Investment Funds and Horizon 2020 in Support of Innovation in Less Developed Regions. S2E Technical Report, JRC Technical Report. Luxembourg: Publications Office of the European Union, doi:10.2760/77101.

6 Foray et al. 2017, see Reference 1.

7 Foray et al. 2017, p. 4, see Reference 1.

8 Foray et al. 2012, see Reference 4.

9 Kyriakou D (2017) Smart specialisation concepts and significance of early positive signals. *European Structural and Investment Funds Journal*, 5(1): 4–11.

10 Charron N, Lapuente V and Dijkstra L (2014) Regional governance matters: Quality of government within European Union member states. *Regional Studies*, 48(1): 68–90.

11 Foray et al. 2017, see Reference 1.

12 McCann P and Ortega-Argilés R (2015) Smart specialization, regional growth and applications to EU cohesion policy. *Regional Studies*, 49(8): 1291–1302.

13 Frenken K, Van Oort FG and Verburg T (2007) Related variety, unrelated variety and regional economic growth. *Regional Studies*, 41(5): 685–697.
Boschma RA and Frenken K (2011) Technological relatedness and regional branching. In H Bathelt, MP Feldman and DF Kogler (eds.) *Dynamic Geographies of Knowledge Creation and Innovation*. London: Routledge.
Neffke F, Henning M and Boschma R (2011) How do regions diversify over time? Industry relatedness and the development of new growth paths in regions. *Economic Geography*, 87(3): 237–265.

14 Rivas M (2018) *Smart Specialisation at a City Level*. URBACT-InFocus Final Report. Available online at: http://urbact.eu/sites/default/files/media/in_focus_final_report_smart_specialisation_at_city_level.pdf [Accessed 27 February 2019].

15 Foray et al. 2017, see Reference 1.

16 Foray et al. 2017, see Reference 1.

17 Foray et al. 2017, see Reference 1.

18 Foray D (2013) Economic Fundamentals of Smart Specialisation. *Economiaz*, 83(2): 83–102.

19 Marinelli E, Tolias Y, Bertamino F, Metaxas M and Grisorio J (2018) Squaring the circle: Lessons from the role-playing exercises on S3 regional and multi-level governance. JRC Technical Papers, EUR 29388 EN. Luxembourg: Publications Office of the European Union, ISBN 978-92- 79-96397-1, doi:10.2760/868791, JRC113434.

20 Barca F (2009) *An agenda for a reformed cohesion policy: A place-based approach to meeting European Union challenges and expectations*. Independent Report prepared at the request of Danuta Hübner, Commissioner for Regional Policy, April 2009. Brussels: European Commission.

21 McKinsey Global Institute (2018) Notes from the frontier: Modeling the impact of AI on the world economy. McKinsey Global Institute. Available online at: https://www.mckinsey.com/featured-insights/artificial-intelligence/notes-from-the-ai-frontier-modeling-the-impact-of-ai-on-the-world-economy [Accessed 27 February 2019].

22 OECD (2018) Job Creation and Local Economic Development 2018: Preparing for the Future of Work. Paris: OECD Publishing. Available online at: https://doi.org/10.1787/9789264305342-en [Accessed 27 February 2019].

23 McCann and Ortega-Argiles (2016), Foray et al. (2017), see Reference 1.

24 McCann and Ortega-Argiles (2016), *Ibid.*

25 Gianelle C, Guzzo F and Mieszkowski K (2017) Smart Secialisation at work: Analysis of the calls launched under ERDF Operational Programmes. JRC Technical Reports, S3 Working Paper Series No.11/2017, Seville: European Commission. JRC106974.

26 Ortega-Argilés R (2012) The transatlantic productivity gap: a survey of the main causes. 20 *Journal of Economic Surveys*, 26(3): 395–419.

27 Boden M, Dos Santos P, Haegeman K, Marinelli E and Valero S. (2016) *Implementing RIS3 in the region of Eastern Macedonia and Thrace: Towards a RIS3 tool box*. JRC S3 Policy Brief Series No. 20/2016; EUR 27956 EN. Luxembourg: Publications Office of the European Union, doi:10.2791/160115

Boden M (2017) RIS3 implementation in lagging regions: Lessons from Eastern Macedonia and Thrace. *European Structural and Investment Funds Journal*, 5(1): 77–83.

28 European Commission (2017) Thematic Smart Specialisation – Interregional cooperation to increase innovation investment across EU borders. ISBN 978-92-79-68858-4, doi:10.2776/713494. Available online at: https://ec.europa.eu/regional_policy/sources/docgener/infographic/thematic_smart_specialisation_en.pdf [Accessed 28 February 2019].

29 Further information can be found at: http://s3platform.jrc.ec.europa.eu/objetives-activities [Accessed 27 February 2019].

30 Radosevic S and Ciampi Stancova K (2018) Internationalising smart specialisation: Assessment and issues in the case of EU new member states. *Journal of the Knowledge Economy*, 9(1): 263–293.

31 European Commission (2016) Vanguard initiative position paper. New growth through smart specialisation. Vanguard initiative. Available online at: https://www.s3vanguardinitiative.eu/sites/default/files/docs/general/vi_position_paper_post2020_final_7nov2016.pdf [Accessed 27 February 2019].

3. AN EXTRA-REGIONAL COLLABORATIVE APPROACH TO SMART SPECIALISATION

1. INTRODUCTION

Smart Specialisation is especially challenging for lagging regions. It is well documented lagging regions are typically characterised by underdeveloped business and knowledge networks and a lack of entrepreneurial talent, as well as limited technological and innovation capabilities. These weaknesses limit fruitful information and knowledge exchange within the region, and constrain the cross-fertilisation of ideas between sectors that are essential for the development of new commercial opportunities.[1] The prevalence of low tech sectors and/or the over-dependence upon traditional declining industries also makes it difficult to identify new 'activities' or 'market opportunities' for policy support.[2] This hinders the ability of lagging regions to fully participate in RIS3 initiatives, and hitherto implement a successful smart specialisation strategy (S3).

In order to break out of this cycle, lagging regions need to look towards establishing paths of renewal or create entirely new routes to deliver sustainable growth? Yet, the question arises as to *how this might be achieved through S3 and within the RIS3 framework?*

One possible route to overcome these weaknesses is through building extra-regional collaboration between lagging and more knowledge intensive regions. Extra-regional collaboration can facilitate network building, knowledge transfer, technological upgrading and enhance entrepreneurial opportunities.[3] However, the incentives to participate in extra-regional collaboration between regions are often asymmetric, and this can pose problems for the design and implementation of policy.

This chapter outlines reasons for supporting and developing extra-regional collaboration between lagging and leading regions. It highlights the difficulties and inherent risks that typically lie within such an approach. We then consider existing European Union (EU) mechanisms to foster such collaboration, and explore these in the context of some illustrative examples from case research in Cornwall, UK, and Puglia, Italy. Both are officially recognised as lagging EU regions, and have been in receipt of significant EU funding. We conclude with some suggestions for policy.

2. SMART SPECIALISATION AND LAGGING REGIONS: THE POTENTIAL OF EXTRA-REGIONAL COLLABORATION

Economic development is strongly defined by the historical capabilities and industrial specialisms of regions. It is important to recognise and build upon these existing resources. For instance, S3 policy in areas such as skills programmes should ensure regional interventions are aligned with local industrial needs but are also geared to local participation in global value chains. Such programmes should also be sufficiently flexible to deal with ongoing structural change.

At the same time, regional innovation policy should also be designed in a flexible way to encourage and promote opportunities for *technological diversification* (see Chapter 2). Specifically, this implies regions should look for potential complementarities and synergies from diversifying into related

https://doi.org/10.1080/2578711X.2019.1621099

technological fields. For example, in Stoke on Trent's ceramics industry, some high end decals firms have successfully exploited their expertise in related sectors including glass, fine art reproduction and high end photographic posters. Other opportunities have also arisen through diversification into 'unrelated technological fields', with ceramics technologies now being utilised in bio-inserts and bone transplants, drug delivery systems and mobile transmitters. Evidence shows that developing new technologies and industries from existing industrial structures can be an effective approach for renewal and regional growth.[4]

S3 policies should also enhance *connectivity* between actors (be it an individual, a company, a government), in order to foster better knowledge exchange and learning opportunities. Historically, policy has tended to focus upon supporting innovation networks within the region. Yet, in the modern global economy, most business and knowledge networks are often organised beyond regional boundaries. This occurs, for example, through global value chains and/or research links between regional actors and universities located outside the region. Indeed, these extra-regional linkages are now recognised as being important to widening a region's access to knowledge and expertise. This is critical for re-energising regional industries.[5]

Evidence at the EU level suggests lagging regions are more innovative when their resident firms are actively engaged with more prolific inventors from knowledge-intensive regions.[6] Building extra-regional collaboration with companies and institutions in more technologically advanced regions might be an effective strategy to enable firms in lagging regions to gain quicker access to new technologies, while opening up new possibilities for learning and knowledge transfer. In turn, this may support the development of innovation capacity within less developed regions. It may also strengthen business networks and allow firms in lagging regions access to new commercial opportunities in international markets.

Extra-regional collaboration between actors on training and skills programmes and/or through extra-regional temporary work teams may also enhance human capital and skills available in lagging regions.[7] A potential downside is if such initiatives encourage more skilled workers to migrate from lagging regions to take advantage of opportunities in more advanced regions. This will exacerbate regional imbalances.

Overall, extra-regional collaboration offers the potential for enhancing capabilities in lagging regions, and hence stimulating the 'entrepreneurial discovery process'. As such, policies to support extra-regional collaboration might be an important complement to RIS3.

However, there is an important caveat in that the incentives for extra-regional collaboration are often asymmetric. While lagging regions may perceive positive benefits from collaborating with advanced regions, this is not necessarily the case for the latter. For instance, the lack of capabilities and technological expertise in lagging regions may dissuade actors in more advanced regions from engaging in extra-regional collaborations. Innovation networks are highly selective, and technologically advanced firms are likely to connect with like minded partners that possess similar degrees of technical competence and knowledge specialisation.

Indeed, research suggests leading regions benefit significantly more from extra-regional collaborations involving firms within the same – highly specialised – technological field. In contrast, in lagging regions the benefits of extra-regional collaboration are more general, and not technology specific.[8]

This suggests it may be preferable for lagging regions to establish extra-regional collaborations with regions with quite different technological specialisms to their own. Doing so may actually open up new entrepreneurial opportunities (as in Stoke on Trent's ceramics industry), which may become the basis for a new 'smart specialisation' to emerge. To foster such opportunities will require a more nuanced application of RIS3.

It is also important to recognise that in lagging regions, limited research capacity in local universities, weak local networks and complex bureaucracy may limit opportunities for knowledge transfer into the local economy. This will limit the benefits from any extra-regional collaboration. S3 policies should therefore also seek to strengthen local networks, particularly between businesses, universities and other public bodies (such as public research centres and public administrations).

3. EU POLICY VEHICLES

Through its various formal programmes, the EU has long sought to promote extra-regional collaboration for innovation. The European Cooperation in Science and Technology (COST) programme (established in 1971) supports international, multidisciplinary networking and collaboration in science and technology. COST projects are led by academic experts, but the emphasis is upon stimulating scientific exchanges and disseminating knowledge to business and practitioners across Europe. One of the remits of COST is that projects foster collaborations between leading scientists and partners from less research intensive regions. The latest COST template (2018) requires new proposals to include at least of 50% of proposers based in designated 'Inclusiveness Target Countries'; these are largely countries in Southern and Eastern Europe where research capacity is lower.[i]

What is COST?

'COST provides funding for the creation of research networks, called COST Actions. These networks offer an open space for collaboration among scientists across Europe (and beyond) and thereby give impetus to research advancements and innovation.'

COST
www.cost.eu

Since 1984, the EU has launched a series of much larger Framework Programmes to support research and innovation, of which Horizon 2020 is the eighth incarnation with a budget of approximately €80 billion (for 2014–2020). Its successor will be Horizon Europe, with an anticipated budget of €100 billion (for

[i] Further information can be found at http://www.cost.eu/about_cost/strategy/excellence-inclusiveness [Accessed 7 December 2018].

2021–2027).[ii] These programmes have sought to develop a world class European research base to meet societal challenges and facilitate industrial leadership, a key element of H2020 is to again foster international (and by implication, extra-regional) collaboration through vehicles such as *Marie Skłodowska-Curie Actions* (MSCAs) and *Joint Technology Initiatives* (JTIs).[9]

The EU's Structural and Investment Funds, particularly the European Regional Development Fund and Cohesion Fund, have sought to foster stronger European extra-regional collaboration as a means to enhance the integration of lagging regions in international markets and mitigate regional imbalances. For example, the European Territorial Cooperation (ETC) programme established in 1990, and more widely known as *Interreg*[10] has evolved to operate in three separate categories of co-operation; cross border, transnational and extra-regional. It has a budget of €10.1 billion (for 2014–2020), which supports over 100 collaborative projects between EU regions.[iii] *Interreg* is designed to be inclusive, and aimed at addressing common challenges through collaboration across a diverse range of fields from sustainable energy, health to transport. Such projects are geared towards fostering and exploiting synergies between RIS3, clusters and network collaboration, and industrial and social innovation.[11]

What is Horizon Europe?

It is a planned 7-year framework programme for research and innovation 2021–2027 drafted by the European Commission.

"The main aims are to strengthen science and technology, to foster industrial competiveness, and to implement the sustainable development goals in the EU."

European Parliament
www.europarl.europa.eu

What is European Territorial Cooperation (ETC)?

'It is one of the two goals of cohesion policy and provides a framework for the implementation of joint actions and policy exchanges between national, regional and local actors from different Member States. The overarching objective of ETC is to promote a harmonious economic, social and territorial development of the Union as a whole.'

European Commission
www.ec.europa.eu

4. EXTRA-REGIONAL COLLABORATION AND RIS3 IN THE REGIONS

4.1. Cornwall, England

In terms of Gross Domestic Product (GDP) per capita, Cornwall is the second poorest region in the whole of northern Europe.[12] This reflects low regional productivity and wage growth; Cornish Gross Value Added (GVA) per job (a measure of labour productivity) is 30% below the national average and wages are 77% of the median level for England. In 2012, investment in R&D was 0.22% of Cornwall's GDP, the lowest of any of the 38 English Local Economic Partnerships (LEPs). These gaps have been widening and make it difficult for the region's businesses to compete both nationally and internationally.[13]

[ii] See: https://ec.europa.eu/info/designing-next-research-and-innovation-framework-programme/what-shapes-next-framework-programme_en [Accessed 7 December 2018].

[iii] See: https://www.interregeurope.eu/ [Accessed 7 December 2018].

This contributes to a vicious circle of low investment, weak growth and poor socio-economic opportunities and outcomes.

The Cornwall and Isles of Scilly LEP (CIOS) have set out an ambitious strategy to address these weaknesses. Vision 2030 aims to raise investment, increase the number of exporting firms from 18% of Cornish firms to 30%, enhance GVA per job to 80% of the national average and raise wages to 90% of the English median level over the next decade. A key facet of this strategy is to draw on the principles of S3 and identify a '*limited number of emerging sectors with potential to exploit new markets and drive growth through innovation and research*'.[14] In 2018, these were identified in a prospectus as '10 opportunities': creative, space, energy, agri-food, tourism, mining, marine, aerospace, e-health and location.[15] While such 'opportunities' may be largely classified as 'sectoral', the prospectus emphasises the cross-sectoral fusion of existing strengths and emerging specialisms, such as the application of digital in e-health, and of marine technologies in renewable energy. On their own, it is unlikely these '10 opportunities' will acquire critical mass, yet that in itself is not

Table 1 Cornwall's New Emerging Strengths and Extra-Regional Collaborations

Sectors	Sectorial Specialism	Regional Assets and Capabilities	Examples of Extra-Regional Collaborations
Traditional	Agriculture	Farming, food processins/Agri-tech/ Artisan food production	Agri-tech Cornwall: international network of food R&D and innovation partners
	Mining	Expertise in mining, engineering and testing (Camborne School of Mines)	¡VAMOS!, MIREU, REMIX projects
	Tourism	Tourism Management/Area of Outstanding Natural Beauty	
Emerging	Advanced Engineering, Aerospace (incl. space and satellite)	Deep space monitoring, space facilitated earth transit, low orbit satellite launch (Goonhilly Earth Station, Spaceport Cornwall)	Collaboration with Leicestershire, Oxfordshire and Solent LEPs on space.
		Civil Aviation, Rotary blade and drone technologies (Newquay Airport)	Collaboration with partners in larger South West Aerospace Cluster (Bristol-Yeovil)
	Marine-tech and renewable energy	Geo-intelligence (Fugro)	Collaboration with Solent, Dorset, Partner South-West LEPs (South Coast Marine Cluster)
		Wind/solar/tidal/geothermal technologies (Wave Hub)	Interreg partner programmers (FCE, ADAPT, PERFECT) on marine, mobility and eco-infrastructure
	Digital innovation: Creative and culture, low carbon living and e-health	Digital expertise especially in creative/ graphic design (Falmuoth Launchpad)	Engagement with Welsh partners: Celtic Creative Cluster
		Healthcare design, innovation and research (Wellbeing Innovation Centre)	Interreg PonTOON partner project to enhance social inclusion

Source: CIOS (2018)[16] and Authors' own research.

Case Study 1 Extra-Regional Collaboration in Mining

Cornwall has a long history of mining, quarrying and mineral processing dating to at least 2,300 BC, yet the last Cornish tin mine closed in 1998, and currently only kaolin is being mined at St Austell. Yet Cornwall retains its mining expertise through its internationally renowned Camborne School of Mines in Penryn, and the Cornwall Mining Alliance, a network of mining related companies and experts based in or with links to the region. This expertise has been the base for Cornish participation in several recent pan-European mining research projects.

¡VAMOS! is an EU H2020 project involving 17 industrial and academic partners from 9 EU countries, which fuses expertise from geology, robotics and mining. It aims to develop an underwater, remotely controlled, environmentally viable mining system to enable the exploitation and rehabilitation of underexploited (and abandoned) European deposits of high grade minerals. Initial testing of a prototype has taken place in both Cornwall and in Ireland and the scientific response has been positive. Success will enable Europe to reduce its dependency upon mineral imports by re-opening abandoned mines, extending existing open mines (which are limited by stripping ratios, hydrological or geotechnical problems) and opening new mines; in each case with limited environmental impact. Several Cornish partners are involved, and the project offers the possibility for them to develop new specialisms in environmental marine mining techniques, each with potential global application (see http://vamos-project.eu).

Similarly, the Camborne School of Mines has taken an active role in two current EU funded projects; MIREU (a COST Acton) and REMIX (Interreg). Both are research networks facilitating knowledge exchange and sharing of good practice between metallurgy regions with different geologies and mining challenges. MIREU is more technologically oriented and largely focuses upon promoting efficient and environmental mineral extraction. REMIX is more policy-learning orientated, and institutional-capacity building; for example, exploring how policy instruments can best support the mining industry, or even revitalise former mining sites into new opportunities, such as at Wheal Jane, a former Cornish tin mine, now a World Heritage and Earth Science Park.

Cornish involvement in these projects has raised the profile of mining within the region. At the policy level, it has led to a re-positioning of the mining industry and the exploration of new minerals as a strategic priority within Cornwall. The possibility of lithium being mined at the former tin mine at South Crofty, also provides Cornwall with the opportunity to play a key role in the future of mobility, the development of electric vehicles and smart energy systems.

This section is based on interviews (conducted in 2018) with senior executives from Cornwall County Council, the Cornwall and Isles of Scilly (CIOS LEP), and participants on various EU projects related to mining.

necessarily the aim. Instead, if properly nurtured, they offer Cornwall the potential for acquiring a more diverse technological base from which new possibilities may emerge.

It is important for Cornwall to develop 'pockets of excellence' in at least some of these identified sectors; this will enable Cornish businesses to link with national and global players, and consequently gain better access to international markets. This involves developing extra-regional collaboration, and working with partners at the edge of the technological frontier. Indeed, CIOS and Cornish actors have been especially proactive in fostering links with suitable partners in both the UK, and across the EU. For instance, Cornwall has a designated Office in Brussels to facilitate pan-European links. Table 1 provides examples of some of these formal and informal extra-regional collaborative links, and their alignment with Cornwall's existing capabilities. Case Study 1 also illustrates how Cornwall has been able to re-invigorate its mining industries through RIS3 and pan-European collaboration.

4.2. Puglia (Apuglia), Italy

Like Cornwall, Puglia (which is part of Mezzogiorno, Southern Italy), has had persistent socio-economic difficulties, with GDP per capita at about 63% of the Italian average. Puglia is the sixth poorest region in Italy, while unemployment is also high, at around 20% compared with 8.5% in Northern Italy.

Historically, Puglia, like the rest of Mezzogiorno, benefitted from the post-Word War II "special intervention" implemented by the national government aimed at spurring industrial development in the South through massive public investment. One aspect of this policy was to induce state-owned companies, especially in designated strategic sectors to establish facilities in Southern Italy. Puglia became a key location for both the steel and aerospace sectors. This programme brought a degree of convergence between the North and the South up until the 1960s. However, it failed to help Southern regions develop their own autonomous capacity – they were largely dependent upon investment from large firms with headquarters in the Northern part of the country.[17]

During the late 1990s, a new approach to policy for the South was adopted called "nuova programmazione" (new programming), which focused on developing local industrial capacity. However, its effectiveness was limited due to tight funding constraints from central government.[18] Over the last two decades, the main action to reduce the North–South divide in Italy has been through European funded regional policy.

As with many lagging regions, Puglia lacks good quality government and social capital;[19] it is ranked the second lowest Italian regional authority in terms of the quality of its public administration.[20] The situation is also complicated by the presence of criminal organisations such as Sacra Corona Unita (a mafia-type organisation). Corruption makes it diffucult to build trust and establish good local business and knowledge networks. This makes S3 policy initiatives especially challenging.

Nevertheless, Puglia has begun to address these issues, by building on both its traditional and new emerging and dynamic sectors. In this regard, it has begun to develop research and teaching capacity in aerospace and also smart manufacturing technologies, especially ICTs and digitalisation.

Through RIS3, Puglia has identified three major technological or techno-productive domains, namely (i) sustainable manufacturing, (ii) human and environmental health, and (iii) digital, creative and inclusive communities. All regional industrial sectors are included in these three categories of activity. Puglia has become active in promoting networking within the region, between firms, education and research institutions in particular, but it also has engaged in a variety of extra-regional collaborations as shown in Table 2 and Case Study 2.

Business and education/research institutions networking is relatively strong. For instance, the mechanical engineering sector has been active in building links with universities, particularly polytechnics that train engineers for these firms. Active university–industry (U–I) links in this activity area have led to the RDMI Hub project; a private initiative coming from the industrial association of the region, Confindustria Puglia, particularly its division in Bari.

The Puglia Manufacturing RDMI Hub was launched early in 2018, to allow regional firms better access to new smart manufacturing technologies and will be one of the 25 European Hubs approved by the European Commission. For SMEs, in particular, it promises to provide assistance and better financing in the adoption of new Industry 4.0 technologies. Partners include the regional government, which will provide complementary measures for the success of the project, as well as Politecnico of Bari – the engineering university of the region which will provide training and research expertise. No Southern Italian region has previously taken part in these types of innovation based collaborative projects. The Hub will act as a network facilitator between regional SMEs and firms located both within and outside the region to provide innovative solutions to particular challenges.

Table 2 Puglia's New Emerging Strengths and Extra-Regional Collaborations

Sectors	**Sectorial Specialisms**	**Regional Assets and Capabilities**	**Examples of Extra-Regional Collaborations**
Traditional	Agriculture, fisheries and Food	Farming, Food processing/Agri-tech/ Artisan food production	ARIEL (Promoting small scale fisheries and aquaculture in Adriatic-Ionian macro region)
	Transport: port and airport infrastructure	Cultural and historical heritage, landscape	INTER PASS (Intermodal Passengers Connectivity between Ports and Airports)
			QNeST (networking of Adrian Ionian actors of the tourism sector to increase sustainability)
	Tourism		Adrion Portodimare project (sustainable development of coastal and marine environment)
	Maritime activities		Blue-growth (networking of the maritime clusters of seven regions)
Dynamic	Aerospace	Aerospace Technological District (synergy large firms, small firms, research centres)	Nereus, network of European regions specialised in aerospace industry
Emerging	ICTs	Smart manufacturing, digitalisation of manufacturing processes	RDMI Hub led by the regional industry association, financed by the European Commission and aimed at diffusing smart manufacturing
	Mechanical engineering		Future 4.0 (Adrion), aimed at favouring knowledge and technology transfer in the triple helix

Source: Authors' own research.

Large multinationals have also been attracted by the enhanced research capabilities of local universities, particularly Politecnico of Bari, which won the 2013 CISCO award for its work on dynamic adaptive video streaming and the 2014 Google Award for designing a new real time congestion control system.

Case Study 2 Enhancing Collaboration in Puglia

Puglia is part of several extra-regional collaboration projects. These include NEREUS (a network of European regions using space technologies, with industry, regional governments, European Commission and the European Space agency) and ADRION and EUSAIR.

In both ADRION and EUSAIR regional policy-makers and other stakeholders are encouraged to collaborate with counterparts in other regions, both in the North of Italy (Emilia-Romagna, Veneto) and abroad, to exchange best practice in policy, methodologies and systems for mapping regional capabilities and to facilitate business networking. These forums also invite firms, especially SMEs, to take part in specific projects and hitherto establish extra-regional links. Universities are also involved in various collaborative projects of various kinds, organised under these programmes.

Within ADRION, Puglia is member of the Blue-Boost project (1.5 Mn € for 2 years), aimed at promoting innovation and cross-fertilisation of ideas in maritime sectors (fisheries, shipbuilding, blue technologies such as green shipbuilding, robotics and new materials). The focus is on creating related technological diversification by favouring networking between SMEs across different clusters (particularly promoting innovation agents such as fablabs, co-working spaces and innovation hubs).

An additional benefit of these extra-regional collaboration initiatives is they are beginning to facilitate an improvement in local governance within Puglia, particularly in enhancing trust among local actors. This strengthens local networks and enhances the possibility for S3 and other place-based industrial strategies to promote regional growth.

5. CHALLENGES AND POLICY RECOMMENDATIONS

Challenge 1

Existing policy frameworks typically adopt a 'one-size fits all' approach to S3 and RIS3, which often ignore the differences between lagging and advanced regions and the different incentives to participate in extra-regional collaboration.

Indeed, lagging regions may be better advised to pursue a more diverse approach so as to explore, experiment and eventually discover their own new specialisation.

Challenge 2

EU funded extra-regional collaborative projects are, by themselves, insufficient to raise the innovative capacity of lagging regions. These weaknesses are often deeply entrenched and may not be easy to reverse.

Policy Recommendation 1

For lagging regions, extra-regional collaborations can be beneficial, especially if they lead to earlier adoption of new technologies, knowledge exchange and enhanced capabilities that open up new entrepreneurial opportunities.

RIS3 and associated EU programmes can play a critical facilitating role in nurturing a broad range of extra-regional collaboration. This can be achieved by connecting actors from disparate regions to enhance science and innovation, while concomitantly fostering better cohesion. Extra-regional collaborations may also endure beyond a typical funding cycle, which, in itself, can help to break-down traditional network biases, and the tendency of similarly minded regions to collaborate among themselves.

However, lagging regions might favour low and medium sectors to search for new technological specialisms and, indeed, these may arise through synergies with different (unrelated) technologies.[21] This runs counter to the prevalent S3 logic, which tends to favour a concentration of funding in specific technological fields.

Policy therefore needs to be supple to allow for such possibilities. There is certainly scope for a more flexible alignment of existing EU extra-regional collaborative frameworks with specific regional RIS3 objectives.

Policy Recommendation 2

Participation in RIS3 and associated EU programmes, not only raises a lagging region's international profile, but can also enhance policy learning at both administrative and industry levels. This is important for both the successful design and implementation of policy.

In Cornwall, for instance, it was evident participation in RIS3 and the underlying principles of S3 have been highly informative in formulating CIOS's strategic economic plan[22] and in pursuing the identified 10 opportunities. Similarly, in Puglia, there is tentative evidence such programmes have been helpful in improving the region's governance and capacity to implement more effective place-based industrial strategy.

Policy Recommendation 3

If S3 projects are to be successful, they need to be supplemented in lagging regions with place-based industrial strategies focused upon addressing structural weaknesses (e.g. low skills, weak networks and poor social capital).

One vehicle might be regionally based skills programmes, geared towards existing sectors, but which also enhances a broader skill set for promising or developing sectors. Such policies can raise regional capabilities, attract new business investment and also enhance the possibility of engagement in extra-regional collaboration.

Mariachiara Barzotto
mariachiara.barzotto@newcastle.ac.uk

Carlo Corradini
c.corradini@bham.ac.uk

Felicia M Fai
mnsfmf@bath.ac.uk

Sandrine Labory
sandrine.labory@unife.it

Philip R Tomlinson
mnsprt@bath.ac.uk

REFERENCES

1 Capello R and Kroll H (2016) From theory to practice in smart specialization strategy: emerging limits and possible future trajectories. *European Planning Studies*, 24(8): 1393–1406.

2 Foray D (2013) The economic fundamentals of smart specialisation. *Ekonomiaz*, 83(2): 55–82.

3 McCann P and Ortega-Argilés R. (2015) Smart specialization, regional growth and applications to European Union cohesion policy. *Regional Studies*, 49(8): 1291–1302.

4 Boschma R and Gianelle C (2014) Regional branching and smart specialisation policy. S3 Policy Brief Series No. 06/2014. Institute for Prospective and Technological Studies, Joint Research Centre. Luxembourg: Publications Office of the European Union.

5 Maskell P, Bathelt H and Malmberg A (2006) Building global knowledge pipelines: the role of temporary clusters. *European Planning Studies*, 14(8): 997–1013.

6 De Noni I, Orsi L and Belussi F (2018) The role of collaborative networks in supporting the innovation performances of lagging-behind European regions. *Research Policy*, 47(1): 1–13.

7 Grillitsch M and Nilsson M (2015) Innovation in peripheral regions: Do collaborations compensate for a lack of local knowledge spillovers? *The Annals of Regional Science*, 54(1): 299–321.

8 Barzotto M, Corradini C, Fai FM, Labory S and Tomlinson PR (2019) Enhancing innovative capabilities in lagging regions: an extra-regional collaborative approach to RIS3. *Cambridge Journal of Regions, Economy and Society*, 12: 213–232, DOI: 10.1093/cjres/rsz003.

9 European Commission (2013) Fact sheet: International participation in Horizon 2020. Brussels: European Commssion. Available online at: http://ec.europa.eu/research/horizon2020/pdf/press/fact_sheet_on_international_participation_in_horizon_2020.pdf [Accessed 27 February 2019].

10 Reitel B, Wassenberg B and Peyrony J (2018) The INTERREG Experience in bridging European territories. A 30-year summary. In E. Medeiros (ed.) *European Territorial Cooperation.Theoretical and Empirical Approaches to the Process and Impacts of Cross-Border and Transnational Cooperation in Europe*. The Urban Book Series. Springer: Cham.

11 Council of European Union (2015) Outcome of proceedings: 25 years of Interreg: its contribution to the cohesion policy goals. 14265/15, Brussels.

12 Inequality Briefing (2014) The poorest regions of the UK are the poorest in North West Europe. Available online at: http://inequalitybriefing.org/graphics/briefing_43_UK_regions_poorest_North_Europe.pdf [Accessed 27 February 2019]. The poorest region is West Wales; see Chapter 7.

13 CIOS (2016) *Vision 2030*. CIOS Strategic Economic Plan.

14 CIOS (2016) p.16, See Reference 13.

15 CIOS (2016), See Reference 13

16 CIOS (2018) *10 Opportunities: Towards a Local Industrial Strategy*. Cornwall and Isles of Scilly Local Economic Partnership: Truro.

17 Polverari L (2013) Policy Rhetoric versus Political Reality: Has the Italian State Given Up on the Mezzogiorno?. *Regional and Federal Studies*, 23(5): 571–590.

18 Polverari, L. (2013), See Reference 17.

19 Antonietti R and Boschma R (2013) Social capital, resilience and regional diversification in Italy. *Papers in Evolutionary Economic Geography*, Utrecht University, n. 18.04.

20 Svimez (2016) *Rapporto Svimez 2016 sull'economia del Mezzogiorno*. Roma.

21 Grillitsch M, Asheim B and Trippl M (2018) Unrelated knowledge combinations: the unexplored potential for regional industrial path development. *Cambridge Journal of Regions, Economy and Society*, 11(2): 257–274.

22 CIOS (2016), see Reference 13.

4. SMART SPECIALISATION IN EASTERN EUROPE: INSIGHTS FROM TWO LAGGING POLISH REGIONS

1. INTRODUCTION

Smart specialisation strategies (S3) work by prioritising regional development spending on each region's distinct competitive advantages vis-à-vis other regions, thus enabling regions to transition into more dynamic and higher value-added sectors.[1] These transitions may occur through regional industry upgrading, diversification or emergence.[2]

Often, but not always, growth opportunities lie in areas of "related variety" i.e. in sectors or technologies that are close to a region's existing specialisations – and therefore make use of existing skills, knowledge and other assets – but are also in some way distinct or new.[3] A key role of S3 is to anticipate the growth opportunities and co-ordinate across various public and private sector actors in order to pursue them[4] (see Chapter 2).

Particular attention needs to be paid to innovative start-ups, scale-ups (growth firms) and SMEs as architects of smart specialisation, because of their propensity to create new economic directions.[5] They, in turn, need healthy regional entrepreneurship ecosystems and bridges to the key 'innovation anchors' in a region, particularly large firms and Higher Education Institutions (HEIs). To identify opportunities and co-ordinate across the relevant actors, the S3 approach recommends an entrepreneurial discovery process (EDP) involving consultations with HEIs, businesses, government and other stakeholders.[6]

S3 received a major boost when the European Union (EU) made preparing a smart specialisation strategy (either at national or regional level) an "ex ante conditionality" for accessing research and innovation funding from the European Regional Development Fund (ERDF) 2014–2020 (see Chapter 2).[7] The European Commission proposes to repeat this for 2021–2027.[8] Various support is available to regions for the design and implementation of S3, notably through the European Commission S3 Platform[9] and RIS3 Guide.[10] Many European regions are actively using the S3 approach (179 EU regions are registered on the S3 Platform), as well as regions in non-European countries, such as Australia and Chile.

However, regions are likely to undertake different approaches in implementing S3. In particular, whereas more prosperous regions will often have a relatively healthy entrepreneurship ecosystem as well as a range of sector and innovation strengths from which they can build, lagging regions have fewer options and need to take larger steps to achieve innovation-led growth and diversification. Lagging regions may also have less policy capacity for implementing smart specialisation, for example in terms of capacities in analysis, evaluation, and networking (see Chapter 2). In this context, it is important to understand both the obstacles that can hinder S3 in lagging regions and the policy interventions along with policy governance mechanisms that can support S3 in lagging regions.

This chapter explores these questions drawing upon OECD (Organisation for Economic Co-operation and Development) analyses of two Polish regions undertaken in 2017–2018: Pomorskie and Malopolskie.[11] The regions are classed as Less Developed Regions for EU regional funding, because of their low GDP per head, and only at the level of "Moderate Innovators" in the European Regional Innovation Scoreboard 2017.[12] They are therefore illustrative of issues experienced in lagging regional economies in Europe.

https://doi.org/10.1080/2578711X.2019.1621100

Using analysis from the two regions, the chapter highlights the importance of:

- Focusing S3 strategies on stimulating emerging industries rather than protecting established ones.
- Addressing regional entrepreneurship ecosystem weaknesses in access to finance, entrepreneurship culture and skills and a basic problem that the majority of SMEs are lacking in innovative capacity.
- Embedding large firms and HEIs in S3 processes.

2. SMART SPECIALISATION STRATEGIES IN MALOPOLSKIE AND POMORSKIE

2.1 Case Background

Pomorskie has a population of 2.3 million, most of which is concentrated in the Tri-city area, i.e. Gdansk, Gdynia and Sopot. It has long-standing industrial specialisations in shipbuilding and transport, shipping and logistics and a growing knowledge intensive services sector. In recent years, Foreign Direct Investment (FDI) has been an important driver of regional growth, with an increase from some 3,000 foreign establishments in 2000 to 5,000 in 2016.

Much of the FDI is in ICT-based Business Process Outsourcing (BPO) and Shared Service Centres (SSC). Pomorskie also has a large HEI sector, with 28 HEIs, including important university anchors such as Gdansk University of Technology, University of Gdansk, and Gdansk Medical University. On the other hand, its research and development (R&D) expenditure was only 1.05 percent of GDP in 2015, with 6,900 R&D employees. It has a high business start-up rate compared to the Polish average and a growing number of start-up success stories, including high tech start-ups, but few start-ups achieve substantial scale.

Malopolskie's population is 3.4 million, including 800,000 in Krakow, the regional capital. The region has significant human capital potential with 31 HEIs and 169,000 students. R&D expenditure is 1.5% of regional GDP, with 14,500 R&D employees. There is also a strong enterprise creation rate in both traditional and emerging sectors. However, productivity is relatively low. In 2016, Malopolskie received the award for Entrepreneurial Region of the Year from the EU Committee of the Regions for having developed an outstanding future-oriented strategy to promote SMEs and entrepreneurship.

2.2 Arrangements for the development and implementation of S3 strategies

The European Commission's S3 guidance indicates that regions should develop both a formal S3 document – setting out an analysis of the region's potential smart specialisations and the expected policy support for them – and actions to engage stakeholders. These processes can be challenging, but the governments in both regions have put in place relevant arrangements. Furthermore, in both cases the resulting smart specialisation priorities are used to influence the distribution of the region's ERDF investments, especially as regards R&D and SME support. Effectively, projects that have objectives, activities and outcomes directly related to the selected smart specialisations are given higher scores in the ERDF selection process.

In establishing their S3 approach, both regions undertook a diagnostic analysis of innovation capacities and challenges based on regional data. The analyses covered current and emerging regional industrial strengths, research and innovation capabilities, and human capital and skillsets.

In Pomorskie, the regional government invited all science and industry actors to a conference and a series of workshops aimed at generating partnerships of actors to propose joint projects in potential smart specialisation areas, including local cluster organisations established in a previous round of EU initiatives. This was very much a 'bottom up' process (see Box 1). This led to the discussion of proposals from 28 partnerships, which were narrowed down to four smart specialisations. The regional government has sought to keep these consortia active through continued workshops and peer-learning events. Pomorskie's S3 strategy was eventually based around two traditional sectors (namely, 1. *offshore, port and logistic technologies*; and, 2. *eco-effective technologies in the generation, transmission, distribution and consumption of energy and fuel, and in construction*) and two new sectors (namely, 3. *interactive technologies in an information-saturated environment*; and, 4. *medical technologies in the area of civilisation- and ageing-associated diseases*).

Box 1 Developing the S3 strategy in Pomorskie

The identification of smart specialisation priorities in Pomorskie was largely a 'bottom–up' process involving the following steps:

Step 1: An economic diagnostic of key regional strengths and weaknesses, accompanied by public consultation and the formation of partnerships.
Step 2: A call for proposals for joint smart specialisation projects to research and industry stakeholders together with conference and workshop activities to stimulate proposals.
Step 3: An initial assessment of proposals by a Selection Board, comprising national and international experts and a public hearing. The selection took into account: global trends, market potential, economic and technological potential, a domestic and international benchmarking, the proposed strategy and action plan, and the potential of the partnership. This led to a narrowing down to 6 specialisations and partnerships.
Step 4: Final concepts were developed by the partnerships for expert assessment and recommendations. As a result, 4 smart specialisation areas were selected.
Step 5: An implementation plan was set up for each specialisation, including its scope, aims, and priority research directions.
Step 6: Partnership agreements with priority access to EU funding were established for each specialisation, subject to renegotiation where needed.

In Malopolskie, the regional government developed their S3 agenda, by setting up working groups on smart specialisation which involved businesses, HEIs and other innovation system actors. The Regional Innovation Council – an advisory body to the regional government's board – also played a key role. The key priorities were three traditional sectors (1. *chemical industry*; 2. *manufacturing of metals and metal products as well as products made of mineral non-metallic materials*; 3. *electrical engineering and machine-building industry*) and four new sectors (4. *life sciences*; 5. *sustainable energy*; 6. *Information and Communications Technology - ICT*; 4. *creative and leisure-related industries)*.

These processes correspond well to the idea of EDP. However, certain weaknesses can also be highlighted:

- The activities have largely been at regional level, whereas there is greater potential for interaction between national and regional government and actors in selecting mutually reinforcing specialisations and in developing joint projects.
- There is insufficient detailed data on locally emerging products and technologies to help identify potential smart specialisations and insufficient data on the impact of different supported collaboration projects.
- It has been challenging to maintain the initial stakeholder engagement because a key motivation for HEIs and businesses involvement was to access ERDF funds, and there appeared to be less chance to influence this once the smart specialisations were established. The momentum of the initial conferences, workshops and meetings also reduced.

2.3. Assessment of the smart specialisation strategies

Both regions have retained several smart specialisation priorities, although there is a clear difference in the number of priority specialisations in Pomorskie (four) and Malopolskie (seven). Furthermore, both regions have included a broad ICT specialisation, akin to a general-purpose technology input relevant across many sectors.

The assessment of the S3 implemented by the two regions under investigation highlights two main issues. Firstly, if S3 is to enable regions to focus investments on their distinct competitive advantages, then it is important to keep the focus tight. Even while recognising that a region may benefit from seeking to nurture a small portfolio of specialisations, maintaining a tight focus is crucial to be able to invest sufficiently in the main potential growth areas. Arguably, both Pomorskie and Malopolskie have too many specialisations and too much breadth in these specialisations. Secondly, both regions have a significant focus on existing industries, and while there could be new opportunities there, they may also be crowding out investment in specialisations with more future-oriented technologies, markets and skills. It could be argued that two of the four Pomorskie smart specialisations and three of the Malopolskie smart specialisations look to the past, with a risk of 'lock-in' in these specialisations.

What is 'lock in'?

Regional "lock-in" arises when collective actions by different actors in a regional economy (including industry, HEIs and government) reinforce a region's traditional industries making it difficult to develop/diversify into new sectors /pathways. It may be reinforced through *ad-hoc* policy.

2.4. Bottlenecks in the regional eco-system and possible solutions

A healthy regional entrepreneurship ecosystem is important to enable scale-ups, SMEs innovation and the emergence of innovative start-up, which play a critical role in helping regions develop towards more growth oriented and higher productivity activities.

Pomorskie and Malopolskie have well-developed business support systems for innovative entrepreneurship, including science and technology parks, incubators and accelerators. These business support systems, however, do not translate into strong entrepreneurship-led growth. This is likely to reflect weaknesses (see Sections 2.4.1–2.4.4) in their regional entrepreneurship ecosystems, in spite of many ecosystem strengths highlighted in Table 1.

Table 1 Strengths of the regional entrepreneurship ecosystems

	Pomorskie	Malopolskie
Business	Business start-up rate and SME density above the national average Large businesses integrated into global value chains and high employment in knowledge-intensive services	Strong start-up community Strong policy support for start-ups (local Entrepreneurship Week, Innovation Voucher initiative, ongoing regulatory burden reduction etc.)
Innovation	Well-developed local innovation support infrastructure (2 science parks, several incubators and accelerators)	Strong public and private R&D expenditures and outputs
Education	28 HEIs providing skills and talent, research and knowledge, and graduate entrepreneurs	31 HEIs and large numbers of students, 13 university incubators
Governance	Good quality regional governance	Clusters supporting strategically relevant sectors, such as video games, IT, cyber security, and outsourcing

2.4.1. Access to finance

Bottlenecks. Entrepreneurs have reasonable access to traditional bank financing in both regions, including access to bank loans. However, it is also important to ensure a range of financing instruments that are appropriate to the specific needs of innovative start-ups and scale-ups, and particularly venture and private equity financing for seed and early stage investments.[13] Although, in Pomorskie and Malopolskie, there are present local private equity investors and a national equity finance programme, Bridge Alfa Investment, they are still at an early stage of development and deals tend to be small.

Potential solutions. In this regard, both regional ecosystems would benefit from strengthening the sources of equity finance, especially for innovative start-ups and scale ups**.** New public support for regional equity funding (including business angels and crowdfunding) should be used to prime and leverage co-investment from private sources. Better connections should also be created with equity sources in other countries as well as broadening the financial subsidy support beyond capital investment. Whilst various existing public programmes offer entrepreneurs financial support for capital investment (machinery and equipment and real estate), there is scant financial support for other types of investment that start-ups and scale-ups often need, such as innovation or training.

2.4.2. Entrepreneurship education and training

Bottlenecks. Entrepreneurship education and training can generate positive entrepreneurial attitudes and capabilities in the young but are currently underdeveloped in schools and vocational education colleges in both regions. HEIs do typically offer entrepreneurship education but it often focuses upon business management or is limited to technology subjects.

Students also have access to incubation space through the national Academic Incubators Programme, but are increasingly demanding more intensive support, including assistance with business plans and mentoring.[14]

Potential solutions. In order to address these deficiencies, entrepreneurship education should be promoted at all levels of education using various forms of delivery (in-curricula, extra-curricular, short bespoke courses, professional training, training entrepreneurs overseas, etc.). A service could be introduced within HEI incubators to help students, graduates and educators think about the commercialisation potential of research and master theses. Both regions could develop the pool of entrepreneurship mentors. In this regard, more resources might be allocated to improve regional entrepreneurship mentoring infrastructures and incentivise large companies to provide staff as mentors to start-ups.

2.4.3. Skills and talent

Bottlenecks. There is evidence of underemployment and skills mismatches in both regions, whereby workers with higher-level skills are working in lower-skill roles and there is a dearth of certain skills, particularly digital skills. Both Pomorskie and Malopolskie lack sufficient capacities to effectively examine the skills mismatches and identify competences for the future labour market.

Potential solutions. In order to address these issues, both regions need to better identify their appropriate skills requirements to better match labour demand and supply. This requires better local labour market data and analysis and a more structured and co-ordinated engagement with training providers and employers that takes account of current and future needs. A mapping of current training initiatives and their directions would help clarify responsibilities and direct existing training initiatives towards new smart specialisations.

2.4.4. SME innovation capability

Bottlenecks. Weak SME innovation capabilities is a constraint to smart specialisation in both Pomorskie and Malopolskie, as evident in relatively low R&D expenditures and innovation activities. Moreover, both regions are shackled by traditional work practices, lack of awareness of co-operation opportunities, and lack of a culture of engagement in knowledge exchange activities with other firms and HEIs. This is despite the existence of existing policy initiatives, such as Innovation Vouchers.

Potential solutions. A positive change would be to encourage SME managers to become more innovation orientated. This will require strengthening management capabilities within SMEs. Increased management and leadership training and dedicated innovation consultancy and mentoring would help SMEs engage in regional innovation collaborations. Help could also be given for SMEs to navigate often complicated procedures to access innovation support and find partners in science.

3. EMBEDDING HEIs AND LARGE FIRMS IN INNOVATION

3.1 HEI–industry linkages

HEIs in Pomorskie and Malopolskie host many areas of research excellence and ought to be regional anchors for innovation; yet, in general innovation linkages between HEIs and business are weak, particularly linkages with SMEs. While some university technology transfer offices are quite active in helping local business to use their universities' know-how and research, others suffer from weak financing and difficulties in attracting and retaining qualified staff.

Both regional ecosystems could benefit through better incentives for HEI–industry co-operation. For instance, academics could be allowed to work part-time on commercial activities alongside their university commitments. Merging allocated university commercialisation funds across neighbouring universities could also create economies of scale and stimulate collaborations across institutions. Regional HEIs could also collectively seek external funding for an investment fund for start-ups and scale-ups.

3.2. Embedding large firms

Both regions have benefited from high levels of FDI, but notable inward investors (e.g. Intel, Amazon, Google and Jeppesen) and larger Polish firms (such as Comarch) are poorly linked into wider regional innovation networks, beyond activities to promote brand awareness, engagement based on corporate social responsibility, or tapping into the university graduate market (see Chapter 2). The concept of *open innovation* focuses on opening the innovation process to incorporate knowledge and solutions from outside a business. However, a developed open innovation platform of this form does not exist in either region.

In order to improve knowledge linkages and knowledge transfer activities, FDI policies need to be more strategic. Both regions ought to focus upon attracting foreign firms that can stimulate knowledge exchange around new technologies. Aftercare of FDI should also be stepped up as a means of encouraging local innovation linkages and support for entrepreneurship.

In addition, both regions would gain from promoting regional open innovation platforms. The regional governments and key stakeholders have a vital role to play in building greater levels of trust in networks between the large firms, start-ups, SMEs and regional clusters in a brokerage or 'dealmaker' capacity.

4. CHALLENGES AND POLICY RECOMMENDATIONS

Challenges

Both Pomorskie and Malopolskie illustrate the typical challenges that lagging regions may have to address in implementing S3. These are summarised in Table 2.

Table 2 Summary of challenges for S3 strategies in the two regions

Challenges	Pomorskie	Malopolskie
S3 strategies		
Smart specialisation strategy process	Public and private actors are active in supporting the regional entrepreneurship ecosystem but multi-level governance of the local science and innovation system needs to be strengthened.	Requires a coordinated approach to innovation and well-defined and informed strategic priorities based on better data. Evaluation of policies needs to be built into policy design.
Developing healthy entrepreneurship ecosystems		
Access to finance for start-ups and scale-ups	Significant support for debt financing of start-ups but early stage equity financing is still limited.	A lack of funding exists for start-ups, particularly private equity funds.
Entrepreneurship education and training	More extra-curricular activities for entrepreneurship and innovation awareness and skills are needed in universities.	Universities should offer more widespread and intensive education and support for entrepreneurship.
Skills and talent	A severe shortage of skilled human resources particularly for start-up firms and for digital skills.	Both high concentration of highly-skilled workers and a growing skills mismatch.
SME innovation capability	Many SMEs lack innovation capabilities.	Few mechanisms exist to facilitate SMEs to collaborate and cooperate and overcome an embedded lack of trust.
Embedding HEIs and large firms in innovation		
HEI-industry linkages	Limited academic entrepreneurship and knowledge exploitation, little SME university interaction. Links between large employers and universities are present, but mostly targeted on attracting talent.	University technologies are not getting to commercial level and HEIs lack interaction with scale-up firms.
Large firm embedding	Better alignment of the Invest in Pomerania FDI attraction strategy with smart specialisation priorities would help support attraction of higher quality FDI. Low levels of entrepreneurial activity among larger firms in the local ecosystem.	Large enterprises have little tradition of connecting and sustaining relationships with entrepreneurs.

More generally, a persistent challenge in many Polish regions, as in lagging regions elsewhere, is that smart specialisation is often not well understood or interpreted in terms of business opportunities and policy prioritisation. Consequently, the opportunity to identify and prioritise investments towards distinct advantages, when compared with other regions, is not always realised.

Policy Recommendation 1

Policy prioritisation needs to be focused and future-oriented. A region's choice of smart specialisation priorities should be focused on a limited number of specific emerging activities with local potential for innovation, productivity growth and entrepreneurship.

In order to enhance this process, regions should experiment with new forms of economic policy governance. Engaging businesses and HEIs in S3 strategy development and implementation is a challenge. The stimulation of consortia to develop projects in particular smart specialisations can support the engagement.

Policy Recommendation 2

Critical to the success of S3 is the regional entrepreneurship ecosystem. Strengthening the regional ecosystem requires:

- Building institutions and networks across government, business and HEIs, which help define a shared vision, mutually reinforcing investments and collaborative actions.
- Supporting innovative entrepreneurship as a key to growth in new specialisations.
- Better exploiting the presence of leading HEIs and large firms as regional anchors and hitherto important sponsors of innovation and entrepreneurship in the regional economies as a whole.

Jonathan Potter
Jonathan.POTTER@oecd.org

Helen Lawton Smith
ubtm188@mail.bbk.ac.uk

DISCLAIMER

This chapter is published under the responsibility of the authors. The contribution of Jonathan Potter is in his personal capacity and the opinions expressed and arguments employed herein do not necessarily reflect the official views of the Organisation for Economic Co-operation and Development or its member countries.

ACKNOWLEDGEMENTS

The chapter draws on work undertaken in collaboration with the regional governments of Malopolskie and Pomorskie and the following additional main contributors: Chay Brooks and Tim Vorley (University of Sheffield); Krystyna Gawlikowska-Hueckel, Tomasz Brodzicki and Stanisław Umiński (Institute for Development, Sopot); Sandra Hannig (OECD); Fumi Kitagawa (Edinburgh University); Łukasz Mamica (Krakow University of Economics); Max-Peter Menzel (University of Bayreuth); Bill O'Gorman (Waterford Institute of Technology).

REFERENCES

1 Foray D (2015) *Smart Specialisation: Opportunities and Challenges for Regional Innovation Policy.* London: Routledge.
McCann P and Ortega-Argilés R (2015) Smart specialization, regional growth and applications to European Union cohesion policy. *Regional Studies*, 49(8): 1291–1302.

2 Grillitsch M and Asheim B (2018) Place-based innovation policy for industrial diversification in regions. *European Planning Studies*, 26(8): 1638–1662, doi:10.1080/09654313.2018.1484892.

3 Boschma R (2009) Related varieity, trade linkages and regional growth. *Economic Geography*, 85(3): 289–311.
Boschma R (2016) Relatedness as driver of regional diversification: A research agenda. *Regional Studies*, 51(3): 351–364.
Content J and Frenken K (2016) Related variety and economic development: a literature review. *European Planning Studies*, 24(12): 2097–2112.
Neffke F (2011a) The impact of aging and technological relatedness on agglomeration externalities: A survival analysis. *Journal of Economic Geography*, 12(2): 485–515.
Neffke F (2011b) "How do regions diversify over time? Industry relatedness and the development of new growth paths in regions. *Economic Geography*, 87(3): 237–265.

4 Chang HJ (2011) Institutions and economic development: theory, policy and history. *Journal of Institutional Economics* 7(4): 473–498.
Gancarczyk M, Najda-Janoszka M and Gancarczyk J (2018) Regional innovation policies as enabling constraints for smart specialization: The Case of Malopolska, Poland. Paper presented to the 13th Regional Innovation Policies Conference 2018 (RIP2018), Bergen, Norway. October 2018.

5 Stam E (2015) Entrepreneurial ecosystems and regional policy: A sympathetic critique. *European Planning Studies*, 23(9): 1759–1769.

6 Stam, E (2015) See Reference 5.

7 Further information can be found at: https://ec.europa.eu/regional_policy/sources/docgener/informat/2014/ eac_guidance_esif_part2_en.pdf [Accessed 20 January 2019].

8 COM (2018) 372 final: Proposal for a Regulation of the European Parliament and of the Council on the European Regional Development Fund and on the Cohesion Fund, Annex IV.

9 Further information can be found at: http://s3platform.jrc.ec.europa.eu/ [Accessed 20 January 2019].

10 Further information can be found at: http://s3platform.jrc.ec.europa.eu/s3pguide [Accessed 20 January 2019].

11 OECD (2019a) Local entrepreneurship ecosystems and emerging industries: Case study of Malopolskie, Poland. OECD Local Economic and Employment Development (LEED) Working Papers. OECD Publishing, Paris.
OECD (2019b) Local entrepreneurship ecosystems and emerging industries: Case study of Pomorskie, Poland. OECD Local Economic and Employment Development (LEED) Working Papers. OECD Publishing, Paris.

12 Further information can be found at: http://ec.europa.eu/DocsRoom/documents/24181 [Accessed 20 January 2019].

13 OECD (2015) *New approaches to SME and entrepreneurship financing: Broadening the range of instruments.* Paris: OECD Publishing. http://doi.org/10.1787/9789264240957-en.

14 OECD/European Union (2017) *Supporting entrepreneurship and innovation in higher education in Poland.* Paris/ Brussels: OECD Publishing. http://doi.org/10.1787/9789264270923-en.

5. TRANSFORMATION AND TRANSITION TO INDUSTRY 4.0: THE SLOVENIAN SMART TRANSFORMATIONAL APPROACH

1. INTRODUCTION

The transition to Industry 4.0 (I4.0) is an irreversible process that countries and regions around the world will eventually need to accommodate. This is because smart automation and digitalisation will bring economic benefits by significantly improving productivity as well as delivering higher quality, time efficiency and customised products and services.

Indeed, Price Waterhouse Coopers (2017)[1] suggest artificial intelligence has the potential to raise global GDP by 14% by 2030. For Europe, Roland Berger (2015)[2] estimate the total potential benefit from digital transformation to be €1.25 trillion by 2025. At the firm level, McKinsey (2016)[3] have argued that the application of advanced modelling techniques alone will improve supply chain management and raise profit margins in the range of 2 to 5%. Moreover, where firms fully adopt I4.0, the average productivity gain is in the range of between 15 to 20%, possibly rising to 30% over time.[4]

Yet these opportunites also bring threats. For instance, automation and increased productivity has implications for the future of work,[5] possibly affecting upto 80% of workers, either by way of displacement, where manual and routine tasks would be affected in particular, or through wage stagnation which is also likely to affect more cognitive and nonroutine jobs.[6] Across the OECD, estimates suggest 14% of jobs are at risk of automation over the next 15 years,[7] although this varies by country/region. In Central and Eastern Europe, this figure is 40%; in Slovenia, it is a concerning 42%.[8] These figures focus on the displacement effects, but ignore the possibilities of job creation that I4.0 can bring. The key question – for any given country or region – is the extent to which they are ready for I4.0 transition.

This chapter considers some of the challenges and policy options at the European Union level for countries and regions to successfully transition to I4.0. In doing so, it also examines how Slovenia – a middle income country – might be able to exploit the opportunities of I4.0, while mitigating the downside risks.[i] Slovenia is an interesting case since it has designed and implemented one of the more comprehensive smart specialisation strategies referred to as S4 (Slovenian S3).

2. TRANSITION TO INDUSTRY 4.0: CHALLENGES

2.1 Repositioning Global Value Chains (GVCs)

The transition to I4.0 is already underway. According to McKinsey,[9] two thirds of industrial companies worldwide now consider digitising their production as one of their highest priorities, and have begun to pilot digital solutions. However, the mass rollout of I4.0 lies ahead and it will be during the 2020s when we are likely to observe the technological disruption of global production systems.

For any region, successful transition will depend upon their re-positioning within global value chains (GVCs), where the "*use of robots, like other forms of knowledge based capital, may allow firms to carry out higher value added activities within the value chain*".[10]

---

[i]Middle income countries are defined as those with GDP per capita of between 75 and 100% of EU average.

https://doi.org/10.1080/2578711X.2019.1621101

Indeed, largely due to I4.0, but also other factors (such as the changing geography of demand, rising wage and transport costs and changing risk perceptions), GVCs are expected to undergo 'seismic' structural shifts. Future I4.0 production is expected to become more complex, rapidly responsive, creative, customised, digital, smart and intelligent, sustainable, with goods and services bundled together, but also more distributed and localised, i.e. to get closer to the end user (see Chapter 6).

The geographic consequences of these changes are as yet uncertain, though it has been argued they may reverse the tendency to off-shore production, and instead bring production back towards developed countries, with production "*increasingly concentrated in regional/local hubs closer to end markets both in developed and emerging economies*".[11]

There are signs this process is already underway. According to the Economist Intelligence Unit (EIU),[12] global supply chains are expected to become shorter and smarter, though not necessarily less complex (due to factors such as, among others, consumer preferences and regulatory burdens). Furthermore, industrial robots in developed economies appear to be slowing the growth rate of offshoring, though for most companies re-shoring remains the exception and not the rule. Nevertheless, multinational firms are reassessing their global operations, and knowledge based capital investments will continue to play a decisive role in the geography of production and the position of regions within GVCs.

For middle income economies, such as Slovenia, repositioning in GVCs will have direct impact on productivity growth. Centrality of a firm, i.e. the extent to which it is connected and influential within GVCs, has already been shown to be associated with higher productivity growth particularly in the case of smaller firms, non-frontier businesses, of firms in smaller economies and in particular in post-2004 EU member states,[13] all features which fit perfectly to the case of Slovenia.

The irreversibility of transition to I4.0 means regions and particularly their firms in GVCs have little choice but to fully embrace the fourth industrial revolution. Failure to do so, will simply mean that regions will be left behind in technological advance. For regions, the focus needs to be upon maximising the potential benefits, while also managing these transitions in a socially responsible way with appropriate welfare packages, to nullify the adverse effects of job displacement on social welfare.

2.2 Raising Investment in I4.0

For each country and region, the transition to I4.0 will depend largely upon its initial starting position and its capabilities. The Roland Berger (2014)[14] I4.0 readiness index shows that middle and low income countries either fall in the group of so called "hesitators", which have relatively strong industrial bases (and fairly benign macro environments), or "traditionalists", which have weaker industrial bases and suffer from inherent structural problems. Both are laggards where transition to I4.0 is concerned, which illustrates the scale of the challenge they face.

Transition to I4.0 will require significant capital investment; for the EU this is estimated to be in the region €1.350 billion for the 2020s.[15] This new investment brings new uncertainties and risks associated with new technologies.

Not surprisingly, the capacity to invest is much higher among advanced economies, with investment in the top third of EU countries generally over three times per capita (per year) as the bottom third (see Figure 1).

If we assume each country undertakes €178 of I4.0 investments per capita per year to become equally engaged in I4.0 transition, then such investment would represent less than 10% of total gross fixed capital formation in frontrunner countries like Sweden or Austria, but as high as 40% and even 50% of all investments in the case of Bulgaria and Greece respectively. Even for the middle income countries, this share would still represent over a fifth of all investments i.e. it would require double the investment rate compared to the frontrunner countries. Raising investment rates in this way is a significant challenge, which will also require double determination and committment.

The question arises as to whether these countries can complement private investment through public support to ensure they are able to transform to I4.0. This does not seem likely as the public capacity to support transformational activities in lagging countries is relatively weak, due to tight budget constraints. Indeed, public investments in Research Technology and Innovation (RTDI) in the upper third of EU countries are almost 9-times those of the bottom third of the countries. Even when taking into account the impact of EU cohesion policy funding, the ratio only drops to 5.3 (see Figure 2).

Figure 1 Total Investment and I4.0 (2008–2015)

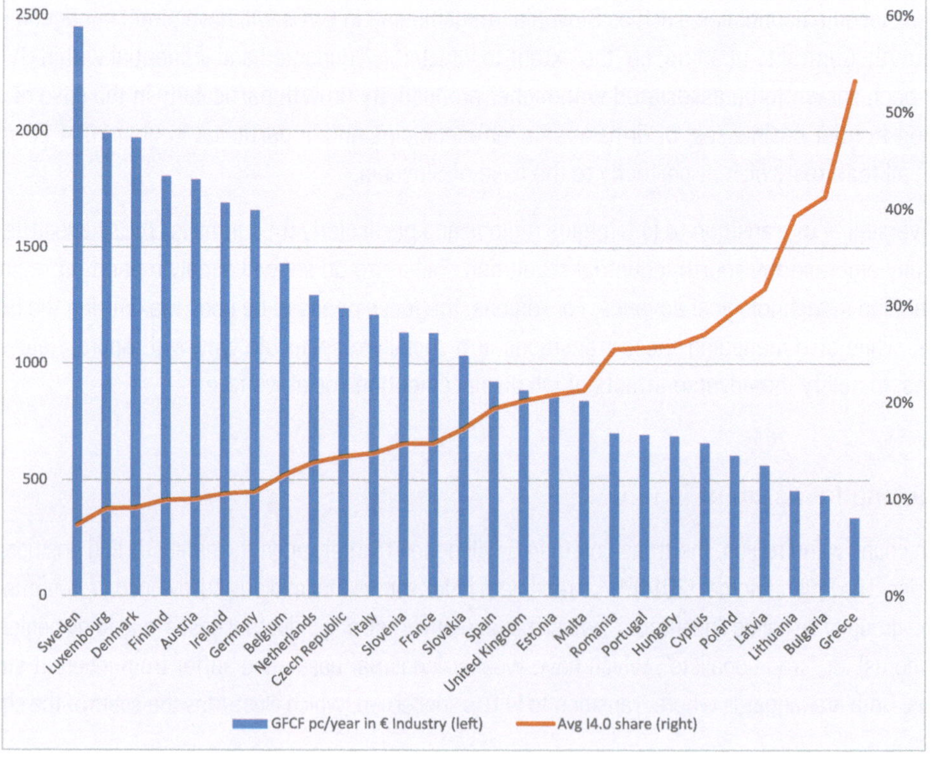

Notes: Gross Fixed Capital Formation in Industry (except construction) per capita per year in € for 2008–2015 period (left axis) and the share of the needed I4.0 investment according to Roland Berger, 2014 in Total Gross Fixed Capital Formation (right axis)
Sources: Eurostat; Roland Berger (2014);[16] authors' calculations.

Figure 2 Public Investments in RTDI (2008–2015)

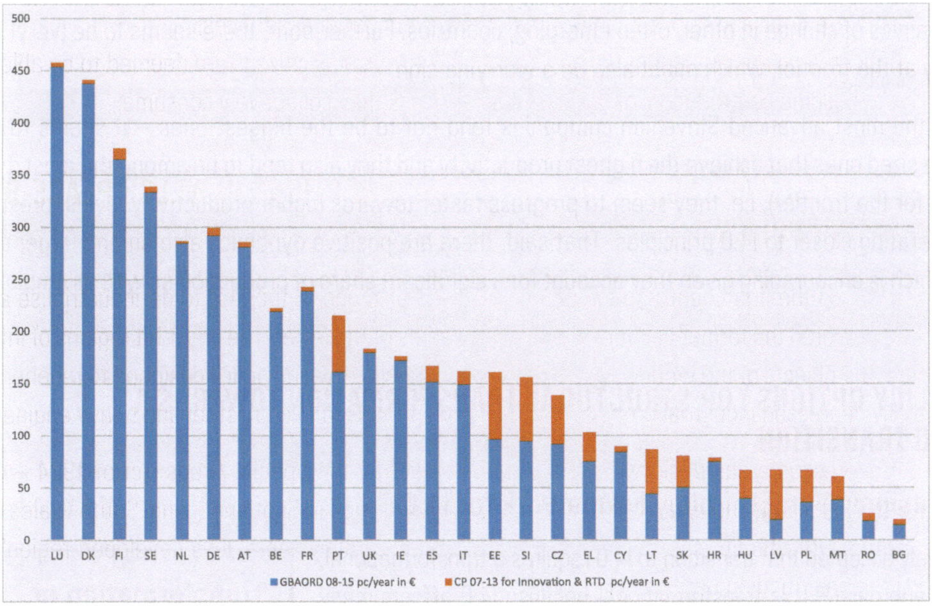

Notes: Government Budget Appropriations or Outlays on R&D (GBAORD) with Cohesion Policy for Innovation & RTD pc/year in €; for 2008–2015 period for the former and 2007–2013 commitments for the latter

Sources: Eurostat; Inforegio (cohesiondata.ec.europa.eu); authors' calculations

In order to assess the magnitude of the challenge, assume that if the EU would want to ensure that no Member States' private sector would on average need to invest more than 10% of its gross capital formation (as would be the case for the frontrunners), then it would need to secure an additional €56 billion over the course of the next Multiannual Financial Framework. This would be equivalent to approximately 28% of the proposed allocation for the European Regional Development Fund according to the European Commission's proposal for the 2021–2027 period[ii] or even less assuming possibility of using revolving funding. Assuming that I4.0 transition would be prioritised across the EU budget as well as at national and regional levels this actually represents a workable solution as lagging countries and regions are not in a position to overcome the challenge alone.

2.3 Transforming the pace of change

The I4.0 transition challenge is also reflected in the pace of transformation and particularly the extent to which firms adopt new techniques and can become more productive over time. The majority of Slovenian firms – typically the smaller ones – operate at lower productivity levels, where it can be reasonably assumed that the principles of even conventional lean production techniques have not been mastered yet. For this group of companies, it might well be that Industry 3.0 (which relates to the widespread adoption of Information Technology and Automation)[17] should be conquered first, pointing to the need for a comprehensive, whole-of-economy approach.

[ii] Based on https://ec.europa.eu/commission/future-europe/eu-budget-future_en, own calculation.

In addition, even though productivity levels increased significantly between 2007 and 2016, the pace of change is markedly slow, arguably too slow given the impact of disruptive job effects on the one hand and the dynamics of change in other, often emerging, countries. Furthermore, there seems to be (very) limited mobility at the frontier, which might also be a worrying sign.

Finally, the most advanced Slovenian companies tend not to be the biggest ones – it seems to be the medium sized ones that achieve the highest productivity and they also tend to be among the most dynamic (except for the frontier), i.e. they seem to progress faster towards higher productivity levels, presumably also operating closer to I4.0 principles. That said, there are positive dynamics also among larger companies, which is encouraging given they account for a significant share of production as well as employment.

3. POLICY OPTIONS FOR STRUCTURAL TRANSFORMATION TOWARDS A I4.0 TRANSITION

3.1. Designing an EU Policy Framework for I4.0

It is widely accepted that transition to I4.0 requires a transformational, holistic approach.[18] It is transformational because I4.0 affects many aspects of economy and society in complex and interrelated ways. Indeed, as Roland Berger (2014)[19] claim, European economies *'are poised to embark on a radical structural transition.... which is much more than "just investment'*. In this regard, it will be vital for future EU policy to focus not only on facilitating the transformation of leading firms and regions, but also to promote adoption by those that are lagging behind.

This requires structural transformation of the EU policy approach to the I4.0 framework.[21] In essence, in our view, this would equate to a policy strategy with the following characteristics:

Transformation or Transition?

The difference between 'transition' and 'transformation' is the latter is a necessary step in order to achieve the former. For example, a company or a region needs to transform itself in order to make the transition to Industry 4.0.

i) Integrated

Better alignment of policies from the EU to the local levels. For example, a better linking of Smart Specialisation Strategies (S3) with EU level I4.0 Action plans and financing instruments (such as Horizon Europe).

The promotion of complementarity and consistency among different policies at all levels. This means better policy coordination – for example, ensuring consistent policy packages on the demand as well as supply side and/or ensuring complementarity between RTDI and HR policies in promoting I4.0 transition. They also need to be comprehensive in supporting the whole development cycle from fundamental research to the market.

Better awareness of territorial differences and promoting partnerships and extra-regional linkages (see Chapter 3). This implies territorial coordination, and making sure cities and accessible rural areas jointly develop innovation ecosystems to exploit different capabilities and synergies.

ii) Focused and targeted

Policy packages need to be targeted on a limited number of key EU (top–down) priorities as well as national and regional (bottom–up) priorities in order to reach critical mass and mobilization of resources.

iii) Structural

As I4.0 requires adjusted regulatory frameworks, standardisation, structural measures, safety net provisions all need to in place and continuously updated.

Figure 3 illustrates how these principles could be translated into action.

It is not sufficient to have an EU vision and goals that would prioritise I4.0 structural transformation – it is also necessary to set up more tangible and concrete *action plans* for more specific areas of activity (such as artificial intelligence or new battery technologies). In doing these action plans should establish links with the other EU policies (and funding streams) through centralised instruments, alongside regulations and standard setting.

Furthermore, these action plans should also feed to the lower governmental levels via modified country specific recommendations, which should represent the link between the EU and national/regional policy levels.

National and Regional Reform Programmes, alongside S3, with their contribution to optimising innovation investments in the EU and promoting new products and services should serve as the integrative mobilisation platforms to enact transition towards I4.0 (across policies, sectors and territories). This should be backed by EU as well as national public funding. Particular attention should be put on skills transition in conjunction with setting up efficient I4.0 ecosystems (see below).

Figure 3 Adjusting the EU I4.0 policy framework

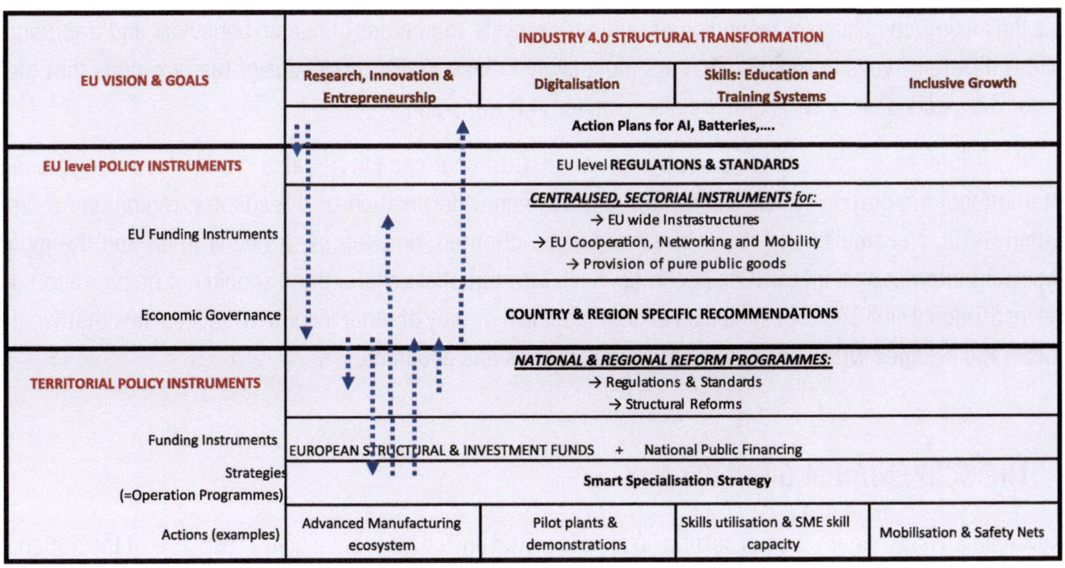

Source: Authors' presentation

The flow of influence should also run in the other direction i.e. from regional governments to the EU level – centralised instruments and EU Action plans should namely take note of the smart specialisation strategies and also jointly promote extra-regional collaboration a well as combining funding sources.

3.2. Building Collaborative Ecosystems and Institutional Capacity

The preceding policy framework would not be sufficient if capability and institutional gaps are not addressed.[22] A key component for I4.0 structural transformation is the development of I4.0 ecosystems built on trust and collaborative networks that encourage the pooling of (human and financial) resources, risk sharing, originality and disruptive thinking.[23]

These eco-systems will become increasingly important as production modes change and '*rigid value chains will become dynamic value-added networks.... within which a network of units will flexibly respond to each other and largely organize themselves*'.[24]

Stakeholders will jointly create value by way of efficient, interconnected and open collaborative networks with trust and social capital representing the glue of the system. Competitors will need to set up strategic partnerships, as they will become more dependent on their business environment, which is especially relevant in I4.0 solutions deployment.

Such collaboration is in practice hindered by relatively high transaction costs (information barriers, time costs of matchmaking). Experience shows that facilitation by so-called intermediaries, such as regional clusters/ partnerships, can be helpful in this regard.[25] Clusters/ partnerships should thus be part and parcel of a network of innovation support institutions that focus not only on traditional issues like skills and joint RTDI projects, but should also network with other institutions that promote ideas creation, experimentation and reallocation.[26]

It is the mixing/combining of technologies, industries, skills, modalities of human behaviors and traditions, across different types of regions, that are most likely to lead to disruptive, out-of-the box ideas that fuel tomorrow's economic growth and are also vital for I4.0 transition.[27]

Finally, existence of collaborative networks and institutional capacity is also the key to strengthened international integration which will in turn (co)determine the position of the country, region and a firm within GVCs. The smaller the region the more niche oriented, on average, it needs to be and the more important international integration becomes. Such international collaboration should not be promoted on the institutional side only, but should be encouraged also by way of other incentive mechanisms that would encourage linkages with highly productive foreign firms and economies.[28]

4. THE SLOVENIAN I4.0 POLICY MIX

Slovenian S4 has a clear vision of setting up an integrated and collaborative policy response at the national level and it has come a long way in delivering also in practice with its estimated 99.5% realisation rate until June 2018.[29] Its main contribution and value added is in:

1. Identification of priorities and relevant niches, where Slovenia has a long term competitive edge at a relatively detailed level (*focus areas, technologies and areas of joint research*), while also promoting technology deployment and convergence of technologies.
2. Niches which are designed on the basis of a renewed collaborative model build on S4 governance structure, whose main pillar represents the quadruple helix type 'Strategic Research and Innovation Partnerships' (SRIPs) led by the private sector for each of priority areas, with whom the government, itself better internally coordinated, closely works.
3. Priorities and Niches are backed up by dedicated and integrated policy mix with special emphasis on skills, RTDI, entrepreneurship, creativity and out-of-the-box thinking, taking particular care of complementarities (on a detailed and daily basis).
4. All activities are geared towards intensive integration in global value chains and interregional partnerships.

S4 priorities are structured into 3 pillars with (S)Industry 4.0 as its strongest arm, with the other two being Digital and Circular – in fact they all three function as overarching directions for change. (S)Industry 4.0 is being supported by a dedicated policy mix, which is illustrated in Figure 4.

As far as technology is concerned the S4 approach has in the beginning put more emphasis on technology development. However, recently a more balanced consideration is being introduced in relation to technology deployment.[30] This is done in a way to ensure policy consistency over time as well as over the complete development cycle.

Figure 4 Dedicated (S)Industry 4.0 policy mix

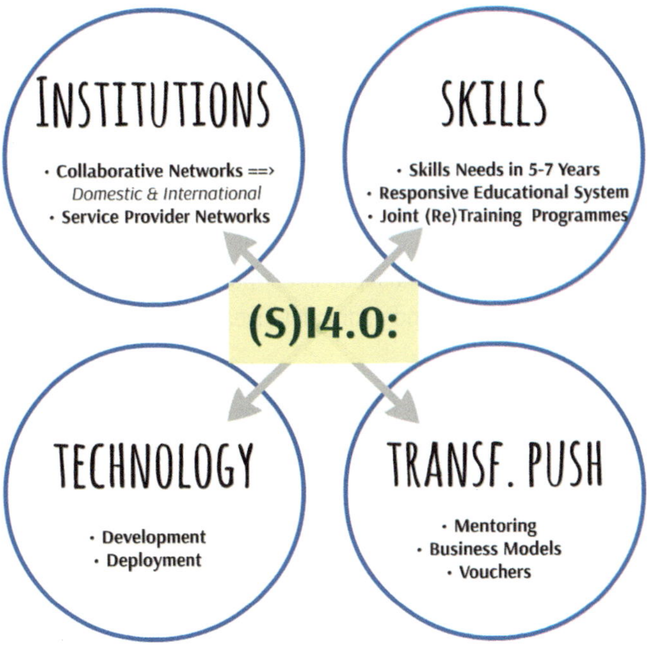

Source: Authors' presentation

Technology deployment on the supply side is complemented with the transformative push for the companies on the demand size. This is done in particular via dedicated mentoring, support for introducing transformative business models (jointly taking into account I4.0 as well as sustainability, circularity and digital transformation) as well as through voucher schemes.

These activities are supported by a collaborative institutional framework that seeks to align the establishment of the I4.0 service provider network and SRIP Factories of the Future. The former's function is in ensuring top quality service for introduction of I4.0 solutions in companies, while the later primarily focuses on technologies and international integration. To illustrate, SRIP is working for example with the Vanguard Initiative pilots and European Smart Specialisation Thematic Platforms to connect Slovenian with the international stakeholders for which also dedicated funding is reserved within the S4 framework.

Slovenian Firms transformation towards I4.0 is matched by an equally ambitious skills transition of the work force. (S)I4.0 approach on the HR side has three key measures: i) long term skills needs assessment to be done jointly with companies for I4.0 transition; ii) working on joint understanding of the future needs thereby setting up responsive and future-oriented educational system; and, iii) work on shorter term joint (re)training programmes, especially of employees, via HR Competence centres that are progressively working along the same structure as S4 priorities.

5. CHALLENGES AND POLICY RECOMMENDATIONS

Challenges

Transition to I4.0 is inevitable given its potential to raise productivity and growth. The most disruptive effects of I4.0 are anticipated to happen on a larger scale during the 2020s.

GVCs are already restructuring and this represents a threat, but also an opportunity for regions and countries, which is especially the case for smaller, non-frontier firms, regions and countries.

Regions and countries have little choice but to embrace the I4.0 revolution and structurally transform to take advantage of the opportunities of I4.0, and nullify its disruptive threats. Yet, different countries and regions have different starting positions and capabilities–however they will all be affected, so they all need to transform. This will require new and additional investment and regions adopting quickly to the speed of technological change.

For lagging regions, both transformation and hence transition to I4.0 is especially challenging and the EU needs to play its role in promoting (and funding) I4.0, which is achievable within the next financial framework.

Policy Recommendations

The required policy response needs better alignment across all tiers of government. In the EU context this means an I4.0 focused, targeted, integrated and structural policy package.

Regions also need to set up collaborative ecosystems and invest in institutional capacity.

The Slovenian S4 approach to I4.0 transition represents a good example of what middle income countries might adopt. However, policy design is just the necessary condition - it is its implementation that will determine who will potentially gain most. In Slovenia's case, if it continues to prioritise and properly fund its S4 and I4.0 transition strategy, then it can gradually expect to get closer towards achieving S4's key mission: to position Slovenia as a co-creator of global trends by setting up of top-level innovative ecosystem.

Sonja Šlander
sonja.slander@ef.uni-lj.si

Peter Wostner
pwostner@yahoo.com

DISCLAIMER

The views expressed in this paper are exclusively those of the authors and do not necessarily correspond to those of their employers.

REFERENCES

1 Further information can be found at: https://www.pwc.com/gx/en/issues/analytics/assets/pwc-ai-analysis-sizing-the-prize-report.pdf [Accessed 20 January 2019].

2 Roland Berger (2015) *The digital transformation of industry.* Roland Berger Strategy Consultants. A European study commissioned by the Federation of German Industries.

3 McKinsey (2016) *Digital in industry: From buzzword to value creation.* Digital McKinsey, August 2016.

4 McKinsey (2017) *Industry 4.0 demystified – Lean's next level.* McKinsey&Company, March 2017.

5 Chiacchio F, Petropoulos G and Pichler D (2018) The impact of industrial robots on EU employment and wages: A local labour market approach. Bruegal Working Paper, Issue 2, 18/4/18, http://bruegel.org/wp-content/uploads/2018/04/Working-Paper-AB_25042018.pdf

6 Further information can be found at: https://www.bain.com/contentassets/fa89826544934e429f7b6441d6a5c542/bain_report_labor_2030.pdf [Accessed 20 January 2019].

7 Arntz M, Gregory T and Zierahn U (2016) The risk of automation for jobs in OECD countries: A comparative analysis. OECD Social, Employment and Migration Working Papers, No 189. Paris: OECD Publishing.

8 Price Waterhouse Coopers (2018) Will robots really steal our jobs? An international analysis of the potential long-term impact of automation. PricewaterhouseCoopers LLP.

9 McKinsey (2018) *Digital Manufacturing – escaping pilot purgatory.* McKinsey&Company, July 2018.

10 See page 22 in De Backer K, DeStefano T, Menon C and Ran J (2018) Industrial robotics and the global organisation of production. OECD Science, Technology and Industry Working Papers, 2018/03. Paris: OECD Publishing. http://doi.org/10.1787/dd98ff58-en

11 See page 27 in De Backer K, Menoni C, Desnoyers-Jamesi I and Moussiegti L (2016) Reshoring: Myth or Reality? OECD Science, Technology and Industry Policy Papers, No. 27. Paris: OECD Publishing. http://doi.org/10.1787/5jm56frbm38s-en

12 EIU – The Economist Intelligence Unit (2017) Rebooting supply chains; Shorter, smarter and more sustainable? A report from The Economist Intelligence Unit Commissioned by Standard Chartered.

13 Criscuolo C and Timmis J (2018) GVC centrality and productivity: Are hubs key to firm performance?. OECD Productivity Working Papers, 2018-14. Paris: OECD Publishing.

14 Roland Berger (2014) *Industry 4.0 – The new industrial revolution. How Europe will succeed.* Roland Berger Strategy Consultants.

15 Roland Berger (2014), See Reference 14.

16 Roland Berger (2014), See Reference 14.

17 Further information can be found at: https://www.coilwindingexpo.com/berlin/knowledge-hub/industry-30-to-industry-40-whats-the-difference [Accessed 20 January 2019].

18 McKinsey (2017), see Reference 4.

OECD (2018a) Going Digital: A holistic approach to policymaking in the digital age. The Forum Network. Available online at: https://www.oecd-forum.org/channels/722-digitalisation/posts/38528-going-digital-a-holistic-approach-to-policymaking-in-the-digital-age [Accessed 26 October 2018].

19 Roland Berger (2014, p.44), see Reference 14.

20 Roland Berger (2014), *Ibid.*

Andrews D, Criscuolo C and Gal PN (2016) *The Best versus the Rest: The global productivity slowdown, divergence across firms and the role of public policy.* OECD Productivity Working Papers, 2016-05. Paris: OECD Publishing.

21 Bachtler J, Oliveira Martins J, Wostner P and Zuber P (2017) *Towards cohesion policy 4.0: Structural transformation and inclusive growth.* Regional Studies Association (RSA Europe).

22 McKinsey (2018), see Reference 8.

23 Further information can be found at: http://www.svrk.gov.si/en/areas_of_work/slovenian_smart_specialisation_strategy_s4/ [Accessed 26 October 2018].

24 Roland Berger (2015, p. 17), see Reference 2.

25 Kroll H, Copani G, Van de Velde E, Simons M, Horvat D, Jäger A, Wastyn A, Pourabdollahian G and Naumanen M (2016) An analysis of drivers, barriers and readiness factors of EU companies for adopting advanced manufacturing products and technologies. Report commissioned by DG Internal Market, Industry, Entrepreneurship and SMEs and prepared by Fraunhofer, VTT, IDEA and ITIA, Brussels: European Commission.

OECD (2018b) Productivity and jobs in a globalised world: (How) can all regions benefit?. Paris: OECD Publishing. https://doi.org/10.1787/9789264293137-en.

26 OECD (2018c) Achieving inclusive growth in the face of digital transformation and the future of work. OECD Report to G-20 Finance Ministers, 19 March 2018.

27 Bachtler et al. (2017), see Reference 21.

28 Criscuolo and Timmis (2018), see Reference 12.

29 For data refer to http://www.svrk.gov.si/en/areas_of_work/slovenian_smart_specialisation_strategy_s4/ [Accessed 26 October 2018].

30 Moncada-Paternò-Castello P, Coad A and Vezzani A (2018) For a transformative Industry & Innovation Strategy. Industrial R&I – JRC Policy Insights, JRC110888; IRITEC Briefs Series – Issue # 5, February, 2018.

6. INDUSTRY 4.0, REGIONAL DISPARITIES AND TRANSFORMATIVE INDUSTRIAL POLICY

1. INTRODUCTION

It can be argued that modern EU regional policy was introduced in the 1990s with the reform of the Structural Funds and the introduction of a clear set of objectives aimed at reducing income disparities across the EU via multi-level governance. The key concern was over a polarisation of wealth and diverging growth paths across different regions: "*to ward off the threat of a two-speed Europe, the EC has reformed the structural funds. The aim is to give the weakest regions the resources to catch up progressively by making more rapid progress than the others, in spite of their handicap*".[1] The rationale of EU support for lagging member states has since evolved over time, from being redistributive at the national level (pre-1990s) to being compensative at the regional level (1990s until 2013) and currently to favouring regional upgrading (2014–20).

The introduction of the Smart Specialisation Strategy (S3) in the 2014–20 cycle has marked a step change for EU regional policy as EU policy has become very much a growth driven policy or a regional level innovation policy. As a new post-2020 cycle is dawning, one can see via DG Regio that "*EU regional policy is an investment policy. It supports job creation, competitiveness, economic growth, improved quality of life and sustainable development.*"[i]

Innovation has subsequently underpinned EU policies, especially regional and cohesion policies. Indeed, the two rounds of Structural Funds over 2007–13 and 2014–20 have seen an increased emphasis on funding destined to R&D and related interventions. Yet, while social and economic cohesion has been a paramount concern for EU policy makers, after three decades of EU intervention through regional and cohesion policies, many regions still have GDP per capita levels below 75% of the EU average. Against this backdrop, the disruptions brought about by the technologies of the Fourth Industrial Revolution have the potential to introduce new layers of socio-economic divides.

Fourth Industrial Revolution (FIR)

The Fourth Industrial Revolution aims to leverage differences between the physical, digital, and biological sphere. It integrates cyber-physical systems and the Internet of Things, big data and cloud computing, robotics, artificial-intelligence based systems and additive manufacturing.

EU Commission

A decade on from the Global Financial Crisis and with austerity increasingly questioned, attention should shift to identifying clear, well-funded and achievable growth targets; however, the EU finds itself firefighting on many fronts, including Brexit, trade wars, and an anaemic enthusiasm towards the EU flamed by populist parties from north to south. The EU risks underestimating the fundamental role policy and public interventions must play just as the economy and wider society are embarking on transformations that will shape work, industry, mobility, communications and more broadly our way of life for the next 50–60 years.

These are times of radical and disruptive change and inevitably EU regional and industrial policies must move towards having a truly transformative power: this could, for example, render S3 with a heightened attention towards the creation and adoption of Fourth Industrial Revolution (FIR) technologies in different regions.

[i] See: http://ec.europa.eu/regional_policy/en/ [Accessed 2 October 2018].

https://doi.org/10.1080/2578711X.2019.1621102

This chapter explores if and how new technologies will widen economic divergence between low and high performing regions and states or alternatively, if and how they might allow some regions to 'leap-frog' with a consequent faster catching up. It also reflects upon the extent to which technological change will require adjustments to EU regional and cohesion policies to allow the latter to have this 'transformative' power.

2. UPGRADING REGIONS WITH SMART SPECIALISATION STRATEGIES (S3)

The concept of S3 was introduced as a new way of tackling regional development. Foray (2015, p. 1)[2] proposed *"the notion of smart specialisation and described the capacity of an economic system (a region for example) to generate new specialities through the discovery of resources and competences in these domains".* The S3 approach has since become the cornerstone of EU regional and cohesion policies and has been implemented through the Research Innovation Strategies for Smart Specialisation (RIS3) in the 2013–20 funding round.

A number of elements of this approach are worth flagging as being particularly relevant.

- One is the aspiration to drive regional upgrading via 'structural changes' that can open up new development paths.[3] With the term 'smart' it is suggested RIS3 must be designed to allow regions to build on their existing specialisations by creating innovation capabilities compatible with such sectors. Framed as sector-specific innovation policy, RIS3 arguably re-invests government with the task of developing capabilities connected with its territory, without being accused of 'picking-winners'. This idea[4] went against the previous tendency whereby policy makers were seen as favouring sectors generally perceived fashionable or desirable, but completely disjointed from their existing specialisations.[ii] However, in reality RIS3 has encouraged regions to upgrade or create a 'competitive advantage' in sectors they already had rather than pursuing a true structural change.
- The second element is the idea of *embeddedness*. Indeed, some form of path dependency is acknowledged whereby *"for many regions, the point is not innovating at the frontier, but rather (to) generate innovations complementarities in existing sectors".*[5] Smart specialisation was conceptualised at a time when the technological paradigm was known and consolidated. The adoption and multiplication in countless incremental variants of the dominant technologies in different sectors and regions were perceived as crucial keys to unlock some form of *specialised diversification* in regions that were lagging behind or underperforming (see Chapter 1). Smart specialisation also drew upon a well-established literature that understood the systemic nature of innovation with its spatial and connected prerogatives. For this, it endorsed reliance on delivery infrastructures such as regional innovation systems with their Triple Helix approach.

[ii] The term, 'specialisation' is in a sense misleading as 'smart diversification' better represents this line of thinking.

- The third element of note here is the *process of entrepreneurial discovery* that would motivate firms and institutions to explore and experiment with different interventions over what opportunities might arise. The novelty here is to envisage that policy makers have the ingenuity and risk-taking outlook – as well as the institutional capacity[iii] – to explore and experiment with policy objectives and tools. In other words, policy design and implementation require some entrepreneurial spirit not only from firms but also from other key stakeholders in the regional system of innovation underpinned by what Foray (2015)[7] calls entrepreneurial knowledge, which can reside not only within businesses but is dispersed systemically.

So, in terms of regional policy, RIS3 has been used to emphasise the need to exploit related variety, build regional embeddedness and enable strategic diversification. This relates to a final feature, notably the need for regional actors (government, firms, universities, research institutions) to collaborate, recognising the current starting point for the region in terms of skills, technologies and institutional governance and then to build on these capabilities rather than trying to start 'from scratch'.

This approach sees the capacity of territories to root their economic activity into the local institutional fabric as being central to their economic success, through the generation, acquisition and exchange of knowledge. Yet such knowledge is uncertain and is embedded in localities; this needs to be uncovered through participatory and bottom–up processes to build consensus and trust. This place-based smart specialisation approach has strong parallels with Dani Rodrik's (2008)[8] perspective of industrial policy as a process of discovery requiring strategic collaboration between the private sector and state in unlocking growth opportunities, but set within a framework of multi-level governance so as to enable a process of local collaboration and discovery.

In this vein, industrial and regional policies which facilitate a process of discovery through strategic collaboration are seen as relevant under smart specialisation perspectives and require appropriate institutions to engender this. Indeed, this is largely how modern, intelligent industrial policy design is conceived of in contemporary debates with industrial policy ideally having the quality of 'embedded autonomy', whereby it is not captured by firms and sectors, but instead focuses on the discovery process, where firms and the state learn about underlying costs and opportunities and engage in strategic coordination.

3. TECHNOLOGICAL CHANGE AND INDUSTRY 4.0

A wave of new technologies is arguably driving a shift in our techno-socio-economic paradigm.[9] These technologies are expected not only to change the organisation of production inside and between firms, as well as the balance between capital and labour, but to fundamentally change the work place, the physical environment as well as lifestyles.

[iii] This can be challenging. See Bailey and De Propris (2002)[6] on the 1988 reform of the EU Structural Funds. This gave EU regions an entitlement to participate in the design and implementation of regional policy but some of the weakest regions lacked the institutional capacity to actually access and implement the funds allocated to them. Regional inequalities subsequently increased and only later started to narrow.

The introduction of these technologies was first noticed in the late 1990s and early 2000s on the importance of general purpose technologies (GPTs) and key enabling technologies (KETs). As the name suggests, GPTs are those with a myriad of applications across different sectors and markets. Similarly, KETs *"act as a platform for the diversification of firms' competencies into a broader set of technologies"*;[10] in other words, KETs tend be to multidisciplinary to the extent their adoption can generate technologies that in turn can feed into diverse applications. Some of the current debate on the FIR suggests these new technologies are indeed KETs. Indeed, there is little doubt on their pervasiveness and disruptive potential. The EU has always been concerned with income disparities but there is evidence there are many factors which can underpin broader variations in access to and adoption of technology, which can subsequently result in wider socio-economic disparities. These include differences in human capital and human capital development, infrastructural capabilities, institutional set-ups and policy, access to finance and culture (including attitudes to risk and failure).[11]

GPTs and KETs

These include micro and nano-electronics, nanotechnology, photonics, advanced materials, industrial biotechnology and advanced manufacturing technologies, as well as ICT and the internet.

- Going forward, knowledge will matter more than ever, so as to understand and use new technologies. However, knowledge is embedded in people and for this it is uneven, cumulative and sticky. Human capital endowments will give some places advantages that others will not have; equally knowledge will age quicker than before, so human capital development cannot stop with education but must stretch into long life learning, training and retraining.

- This takes us to the second discriminating factor; infrastructural capability, which includes education and innovation systems. These again can vary greatly in quality and content although the EU has made huge progress in aligning qualifications to enable frictionless labour mobility across EU member states.

- The EU has favoured the conservation of national and regional institutional set ups and policy frameworks to reflect the peculiarity of member states. This was very much endorsed by the subsidiarity principle adopted as a corner stone of the Reform of Structural Funds. This means the mechanisms for change that are driven by policy and institutions also vary greatly. In terms of access to finance, for example, firms face a more similar landscape: according to Hundley et al. (2003)[12] the EU overall lacks risk capital to facilitate new and innovative firms' formation especially at times of high risk such as when technology is changing. This goes hand in hand with an overall greater attitude towards risk aversion than in the USA for instance (*ibid*).

Across EU member states and regions there are clear divides and a major issue for EU policy makers is to what extent technological change will lock regions into some path dependency development that will ultimately exacerbate such cleavages.

Serious concerns have been raised about the risk of so-called digital divides which can emerge between regions in the same country, between countries and more crucially between the rich and poor in society. We focus here on cross-country divides that technological change can trigger. There are many factors

Figure 1 Enterprises that employ ICT specialists, percentage of enterprises

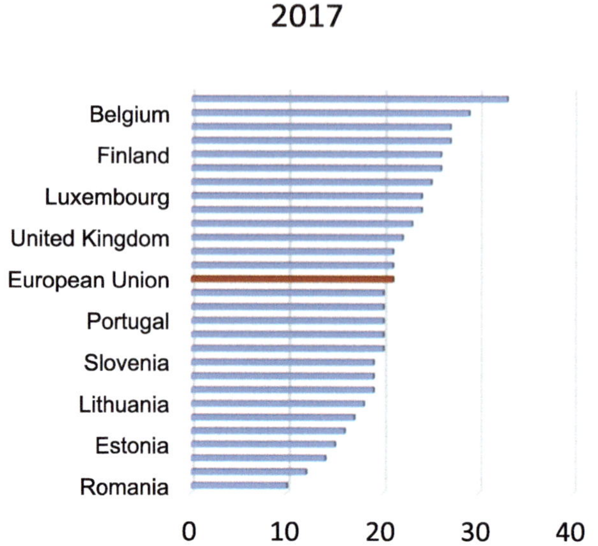

Source: Our elaboration from Eurostat.

causing digital divides and these include differences in human capital and human capital development, infrastructural capabilities, institutional set-ups and policy, access to finance and culture (including attitudes to risk and failure).

The EU Regional Innovation Scoreboard (2017) allows us to clearly identify certain innovation leaders and laggards across the EU. Two indicators are especially indicative of the complexity of the situation. If we take the number of firms across EU member states employing ICT specialists as a proxy for digital skills, a clear divide emerges between northern European countries and southern and eastern ones (see Figure 1).[iv]

Equally, considering the level of automation and digitalisation in the production process, countries characterised by industries reliant on scale economies and which are therefore larger in size (such as in Germany) tend to have a greater number of enterprises whose business processes are already automatically linked to suppliers/customers. This can of course deliver greater efficiency and labour productivity (see Figure 2).

Finally, the degree of digital penetration can be measured by people's digital skills.[v] Data shows the picture is quite different; core EU countries show much less digital dexterity than Italy, Spain, UK and the Scandinavia economies (see Figure 3). The reasons might be manifold, including the extent of infrastructural investment and societal readiness.

[iv] Enterprises with at least 10 employees, NACE sectors, 2009–2017.

[v] Internet skills are measured using a self-assessment approach, depending on how many internet related tasks have been carried out, without these skills being assessed, tested or actually observed. 5 or 6 of the following activities have been done: used search engine, sent mail with attachment, posted messages to chatrooms/newsgroups or online discussion forum, made phone calls, done peer-to-peer file sharing or created a web page. Individuals ages 16–74. Year 2013.

Figure 2 Enterprises whose business processes are automatically linked to suppliers/customers

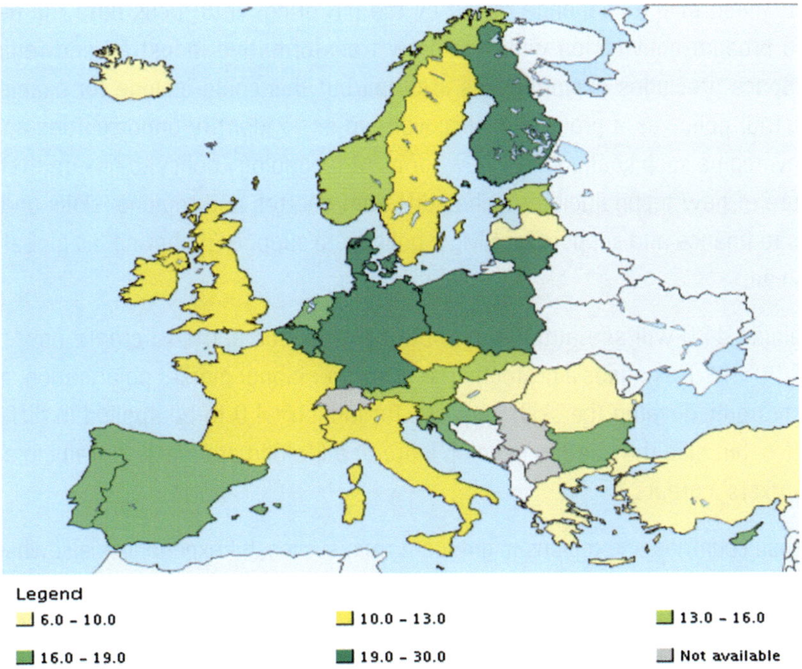

Source: Our elaboration from Eurostat

Figure 3 Internet skills

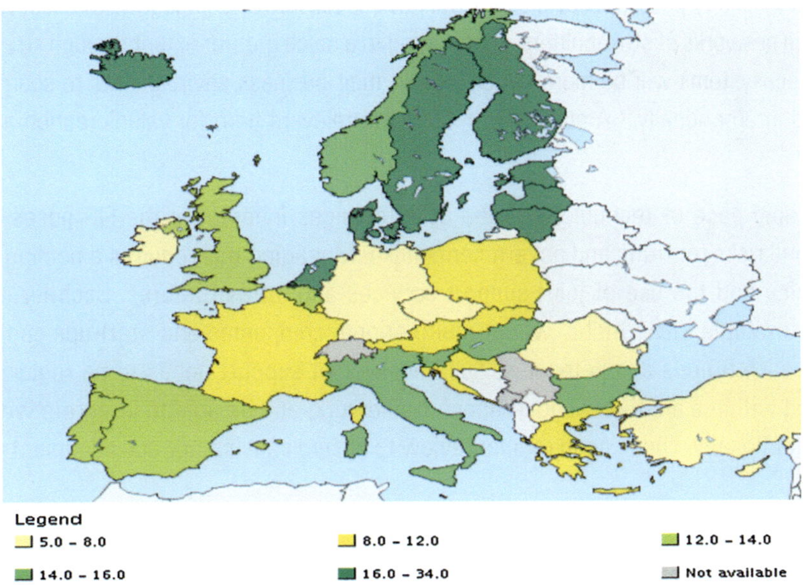

Source: Our elaboration from Eurostat

4. TOWARDS A NEW, TRANSFORMATIVE INDUSTRIAL POLICY

The scale and speed of the challenge posed by the FIR brings into focus both the need and possibilities for a broader canvass on which to draw transformative industrial and regional policies approaches. Space precludes exploring this in detail but this could include for example: fostering regional industrial policy as a process of discovery so as to identify opportunities and challenges and ways to overcome such challenges;[13] new forms of technology policy to ensure that the 'general purpose' nature of new technologies reaches different sectors and regions; skills and (re-)training policy; access to finance and support for SMEs; policies to support 'reshoring' as global value chains change and so on.

Firstly, on training, I4.0 will see automation both destroy jobs and also create new ones (see for example WEF, 2018)[14]. This raises a profound risk of further labour market polarisation, and there will be a need to not only develop the skills required for Industry 4.0 to be applied in different sectors and regions also, but also the need to develop more of a lifelong approach to training and retraining throughout workers' careers.

On this, European countries and regions might learn from successful experiences elsewhere, such as in Singapore with its 'Skills Future' programme as well as regional examples in the EU itself. An instructive reginal example is Emilia-Romagna, particularly through its 2015 '*Patto per il Lavoro*' (Pact for Employment and Growth).[15] The pact lays out a long-term vision for regional development, comprising a shared understanding of challenges and a joint approach to foster investment, growth and better jobs, with interventions to leverage the region's strategic assets.

Secondly on technology policy, policy makers will have to nurture and engage with ecosystems of open, interconnected networks of stakeholders, cooperating to a much greater extent through strategic partnerships.[16] Such ecosystems will be more dependent on their business environments to source knowledge regionally and internationally.[17] A number of factors are relevant here for value creation and capture in ecosystems.[18]

Thirdly, the rapid pace of technological and other changes inherent in the FIR poses considerable uncertainty and risks for firms and governments alike. Managing this requires a pooling of resources and risk-sharing and the use of joint support services and infrastructures. Bachtler et al. (2017)[19] highlight, for example, 'living-labs' where multinational companies and start-ups can interact and benefit from each other's competencies. Such ecosystem support needs to be regionally provided but positioned within a multi-level governance framework, and be able to integrate with innovation systems internationally. These need regular review to ensure consistency and alignment with regional demands.

Fourthly, disruptive innovation often requires inter-disciplinary approaches and 'open' models of collaboration.[20] As the OECD (2017)[21] notes, "*pieces of knowledge required come from various actors and activities are rarely available inside a single organisation… it is important therefore to support the generation, diffusion and use of many sorts of knowledge and types of collaboration"*. For this 'mixing' to occur, an open and collaborative environment is needed, built upon established relationships and trust. This in turn highlights the need for well-developed institutions capable of nurturing collaboration and networks both regionally and internationally and in industrial policy terms in bringing actors together in the knowledge discovery process.

Finally, as global value chains change and small-scale production possibilities emerge again, there may be scope for industrial policy to help 'repopulate' manufacturing ecosystems in the UK and Europe. For instance, consider 'home sourcing' in Spanish manufacturing, where policy may well have a role to play, but not in trying to bring back labour-intensive activities, which will in any case be susceptible to wage/exchange rate shifts (and are footloose in nature as relative unit labour costs shift). Instead, recent Spanish experiences suggest activities undertaken by R&D-intensive manufacturing firms producing non-standardised products are more likely to be re-shored.[22] Reshoring is unlikely to re-create large numbers of manufacturing jobs and certainly not low-skilled jobs that have been offshored or outsourced abroad.

In addition, while reshoring as global value chains change is indeed a real opportunity, it is not a foregone conclusion, since actual logistics can be challenging.[23] Whether reshoring benefits mature EU regions will depend – inter alia – on the availability of skills, innovation capacity, the supply chain base, support services and the role of institutions. Maintaining an ecosystem of firms and agencies provides firms with a 'deal-breaking' anchor, making home-sourcing a viable option (this correlates to recent US and British reshoring experiences).

5. CHALLENGES AND POLICY RECOMMENDATIONS

Challenge 1

The generic challenge for the forthcoming round of RIS3 will be to acknowledge the transformative necessity of policy intervention as against a more incremental upgrading approach, which has tended to dominate previous policy frameworks.

Furthermore, a transformative industrial strategy needs to be developed both nationally and regionally in a holistic sense (for example on skills, access to finance, clusters, supply chains and innovation) so as to enable policy to be better suited to the distinctive characteristics and advantages of different scales.

Challenge 2

As the FIR will play out differently across sectors and regions, this will bring new challenges for the focus of and the innovation aspirations of EU cohesion policy.

The integration of sectors with new technologies will be fundamental in allowing the former to be truly transformed in the light of the new technologies. The challenge for a truly transformative industrial policy is to design an integrative and flexible policy framework that 'joins up' technologies, sectors and places.

Policy Recommendation 1

Policy interventions should form part of a more holistic industrial strategy for stimulating business investment and new firm formation to rebuild value creation and capture, and safeguard manufacturing ecosystem competitiveness. Policy needs to take this on board, for example in private-public-sector dialogue to identify opportunities to re-join supply chain functions.

This reflects modern conceptions of industrial policy as a collaborative process of discovery of information involving the public and private sector.

Policy Recommendation 2

A transformative industrial policy needs to think beyond sectors alone, and rather identify, nurture and diffuse the key cross-cutting technologies (e.g. digitalisation, internet of things, robotics and artificial intelligence) that have an enabling role across manufacturing and services.

Linked to this, industrial strategy needs to recognise and exploit such technologies by making them accessible to businesses in different regions. This could entail examining what a regional industrial strategy might look like, identifying sectoral trends, analysing emerging strengths and opportunities identified, and carrying out analysis of the export potential of key sectors in which the region already holds emergent strengths and which can be built on in a 'smart specialisation' sense.

Policy Recommendation 3

Critical to this process are regionally-based industrial development strategies promoting 'related diversification' capitalising on the FIR. Such strategies need to recognise

- the need to bring together different but related activities in a region via cross cutting FIR technology platforms (e.g. via Living Labs or digital demonstration hubs) and
- the differing potentials of regions to diversify, due to different industrial, knowledge and institutional structures linked to specific regional historical trajectories. Rather than 'starting from scratch' or applying 'one size fits all policies', regional industrial strategies for the FIR instead require tailor-made policy actions embedded in, and linked to the specific needs and available resources of regions, starting with the existing knowledge and institutional base in that region. These need to capitalise on region-specific assets, rather than attempting to replicate and apply policies that may have worked in quite different places.

Policy Recommendation 4

In order to transform the region's potential and enabling it branch into new related activities, policy could encourage crossovers between manufacturing (and service) industries and between manufacturing and new technologies. This could come via knowledge transfer mechanisms that connect related and unrelated industries, such as by:

- enhancing entrepreneurship from unrelated industries (targeting such entrepreneurs would not only increase the likelihood of successful policy, but could also contribute to regional diversification);
- encouraging labour mobility between related and unrelated industries, as it transfers knowledge between industries and may lead to new 'recombinations' of knowledge (such labour mobility could also increase the level of human capital, as firms and employees learn from experience in related sectors and in turn helps regional resilience as workers can move between sectors);
- promoting exposure to new technologies via institutional intermediaries;
- supporting collective research collaboration with partners from related and unrelated competences.

Other elements would involve, inter alia, the need for: new skills to be developed and constant re-skilling and up-skilling processes as the FIR progresses; enabling SMEs to have access to funding and finance to embrace digital technologies; recognising and exploiting possibilities to reposition firms, industries and regions on new parts of the global value chain as the value added of manufacturing changes over time; seizing re-shoring opportunities as relocalisation opportunities open up – involving policies to rebuild supply chains in Europe; infrastructure investment to embrace new technologies (e.g. 5G) and so on as part of an holistic regional industrial policy.

David Bailey
D.G.BAILEY@bham.ac.uk

Lisa De Propris
L.DEPROPRIS@bham.ac.uk

ACKNOWLEDGEMENTS

The writing of this paper has been supported by the EU Horizon 2020 project MAKERS – Smart Manufacturing for EU growth and prosperity is a project funded by the Horizon 2020 Research and Innovation Staff Exchange Programme, which is a Research and Innovation Staff Exchange under the Marie Sklodowska-Curie Actions, grant agreement number 691192. David Bailey also acknowledges support from the Economic and Social Research Council *UK in a Changing Europe* Programme UK [grant reference: ES/T000848/1]. Ethical disclaimer: the secondary data used in the paper was collected before the MAKERS project.

REFERENCES

1 See page 10 in European Commission (1992) Reform of the structural funds: A tool to promote economic and social cohesion. Luxembourg: Office for Official Publications of the European Communities.

2 Foray D. (2015) *Smart Specialisation*. Routledge: London.

3 See page 39 in Foray D (2017) The economic fundamentals of smart specialization strategies. In S Radosevic, A Curaj, R Gheorghiu, L Andreescu and I. Wade (eds) *Advances in the Theory and Practice of Smart Specialization*, pp. 37–50. London: Elsevier.

4 Foray (2015), see Reference 2.

5 Foray (2017, p. 47), see Reference 3.

6 Bailey D and De Propris L (2002) The 1988 reform of the structural funds: entitlement or empowerment?. *Journal of European Public Policy*, 9(3): 408–428.

7 Foray (2015), see Reference 2.

8 Rodrik D (2008) *One Economics, Many Recipes: Globalization, Institutions, and Economic Growth*. Princeton, NJ: Princeton University Press.

9 Perez C (2010) Technological revolutions and techno-economic paradigms. *Cambridge Journal of Economics*, 34(1): 185–202.

10 See page 198 in Corradini C and De Propris L (2017) Beyond local search: Bridging platforms and inter-sectoral technological integration. *Research Policy*, 46(1): 196–206.

11 Hundley R, Anderson RH, Bikson TK and Neu CR (2003) *The Global Course of the Information Revolution: Recurring Themes and Regional Variations*. Santa Monica, CA: Rand Corporation.

12 Hundley et al. (2003), see Reference 11.

13 Rodrik D (2004) *Industrial Policy for the 21st Century*. Cambridge, MA: John F Kennedy School of Government. Rodrik (2008), see Reference 8.

14 WEF (World Economic Forum) (2018) *The future of jobs report 2018*. http://www3.weforum.org/docs/WEF_Future_of_Jobs_2018.pdf [Accessed 20 January 2019].

15 Bianchi P and Labory S (2018) *Industrial Policy for the Manufacturing Revolution. Perspectives on Digital Globalisation*. Cheltenham: Edward Elgar.

16 Bachtkler J, Martins JO, Wostner P and Zuber P (2017) *Towards Cohesion Policy 4.0. Structural Transformation and Inclusive Growth*. Brussels: RSA Europe.

17 Roland Berger (2015) The digital transformation of industry. Roland Berger Strategy Consultants. A European study commissioned by the Federation of German Industries.

18 Bailey D, Pitelis C and Tomlinson P (2018) A place-based developmental regional industrial strategy and/for sustainable capture of co-created value. *Cambridge Journal of Economics*, 6(9): 1521–1542.

19 Bachtler et al. (2017), see Reference 16.

20 Chesbrough HW (2003) The era of open innovation. *MIT Sloan Management Review*, 44(3): 35–41.

21 See page 68 in OECD (2017) The next production revolution: Implications for governments and business. Paris: OECD Publishing.

22 Bailey D, Corradini C and De Propris L. (2018) 'Home-sourcing' and closer value chains in mature economies: The case of Spanish manufacturing. *Cambridge Journal of Economics*, 6(9): 1567–1584.

23 Bailey D and De Propris L (2014) Manufacturing reshoring and its limits: The UK automotive case. *Cambridge Journal of Regions, Economy and Society*, 7(3): 379–398.

7. THE FUTURE OF PLACE-BASED INNOVATION POLICY (AS IF 'LAGGING REGIONS' REALLY MATTERED)

1. INTRODUCTION

The place-based approach championed by the Barca Report[1] is almost ten years old and its most famous expression, Smart Specialisation Strategy (S3), is being implemented in and beyond the European Union (EU). This chapter reflects upon recent experience and speculates on the future prospects of S3 as the flagship of place-based innovation policy. In doing so, this chapter offers an interpretation of S3 which suggests it harbours a schizophrenic conception of innovation: that is to say, it contains an explicit model of innovation based on Science and Technology (S&T) as well as an implicit model based on Social Innovation.

The focus here is grounded in the Foundational Economy (FE) perspective, a radically new place-based approach to local development.[2] In contrast to the S&T model, which tends to favour a small band of advanced technology sectors, the overriding concern of the FE perspective is to raise the economic status and political visibility of the *"mundane sectors"* that help to keep people and places *"safe, sound and civilised"*; sectors such as health, education, dignified eldercare and food for example.

It is in 'lagging regions' where place-based policies such as S3 face their biggest challenges. In this regard, certain lagging regions are beginning to re-invent themselves by framing their place-based innovation policies in more capacious ways so as to embrace rather than exclude the people and places *'that have been left behind'*.[3] To illustrate the point the chapter highlights the recent experience of Wales, which hosts the largest 'less developed region' in the UK, but which also happens to be the first country to incorporate the FE perspective into its place-based policy repertoire.

2. THE NEW CONCEPTUAL LANDSCAPE OF INNOVATION

The conventional S&T model of innovation is giving way to new conceptions in which social innovation, place-based innovation, smart cities and mission-led innovation oblige us to re-consider what 'innovation' actually means today and who are the principal agents of innovation.

Although business remains a key driver of innovation, it is increasingly recognised that other agents are also important. These include social enterprises and grassroots organisations in the case of social innovation; regional governments and their ecosystem partners in the case of place-based innovation; urban municipalities in the case of 'smart' cities; consumers in the case of user-driven innovation; urban living labs in the case of sustainability transitions; and a wide array of social agents such as Non-Governmental Organisations (NGOs) in the case of mission-led innovation programmes that are designed to address societal challenges such as climate change, renewable energy, healthy ageing and food security.[4]

What is social innovation?

Social Innovations are new ideas, products and services which address unmet social challenges (e.g. healthy ageing/climate change) and create new social relationships/ collaborations.

EU Commission (2010)

https://doi.org/10.1080/2578711X.2019.1621103

It was in this context that the S3 concept was designed and later developed into a set of policy prescriptions in the RIS3 Guide.[5] However, the Guide itself contains a somewhat schizophrenic attitude to innovation which can be explained, at least in part, by the changing landscape of innovation studies. The conventional approach of the S&T model almost exclusively focuses upon promoting knowledge-generating sectors and is largely framed in instrumentalist terms; *a means to an end and the end in question is greater economic competitiveness*. As such it has come to dominate place-based innovation policy.

Yet, the RIS3 Guide itself is framed more broadly than this, since S3;

> *"embraces a broader concept of innovation, not only investment in research or the manufacturing sector, but also building competitiveness through design and creative industries, social and service innovation, new business models and practice-based innovation"*.[6]

From this, we might infer a more implicit model of innovation – a socio-ecological model – with very different ends. These ends are not instrumentally tied to delivering economic competitiveness, but rather geared *intrinsically towards the significant* ends of human needs *(e.g. health, education, social care)* and environmental sustainability. We would argue this model needs to be given more prominence.

Indeed, the Guide also notes *'social innovation is important for regional development'* because, as well as creating new business opportunities, it can *'provide new perspectives to citizens, and help the modernisation of the public sector'*. The Guide is also clear that the public sector *'has a pivotal role in answering today's major societal challenges such as demographic ageing, increased demand for healthcare services, risk of poverty and social exclusion'*.[7]

If the socio-ecological model of innovation was endorsed by the official S3 Guide – albeit implicitly – why were social innovation projects not more widely targeted for funding when it came to putting S3 into practice? The Guide proved to be highly prescient when it anticipated some of the barriers to this implicit model of innovation:

> *Social innovation is a relatively new concept… There is a risk of it being hampered by insufficient knowledge, limited support of grass roots… poor diffusion and little scale-up of good practices and poor methods of impact evaluation*.[8]

Above all, the Guide notes social innovation requires a *'considerable mentality change'*. Indeed, the concept itself is highly contested and malleable, and as such it has been appropriated by a wide range of causes, conservative as well as radical.[9] One of these radical causes is the Foundational Economy, a social innovation strategy that focuses on *'the infrastructure of everyday life'* (see Section 4).[10]

3. HORIZON EUROPE AND THE FUTURE EU INNOVATION POLICY

How will the tension between these two models of innovation – the explicit S&T model and the implicit socio-ecological model – play out in future?

The future direction of research and innovation policy in the EU has already been outlined by the European Commission (EC) in its proposed budget allocation for Horizon Europe (Figure 1), the successor to the current Horizon 2020 programme, which has been provisionally allocated EUR 97.6 billion for the 2021–2027 programming period.[11]

Figure 1 Horizon Europe: The proposed research and innovation programme (2021–2027)

Pillar 2 has been allocated the lion's share of the budget, accounting for EUR 52.7 billion, and this is where the proposed 'mission-oriented' Research and Innovation (R&I) projects are most likely to be found. According to the EC, these R&I missions will include '*bold goals to tackle issues that affect our daily lives*'.

Examples could range from the fight against cancer, to clean transport or plastic-free oceans. They will be co-designed with citizens, stakeholders, the European Parliament and Member States. Assuming they are confirmed, these proposals suggest the two models of innovation outlined above will become ever more intertwined because it is difficult, if not impossible, to imagine R&I projects addressed to societal challenges – *like healthcare, eldercare, mobility, low-carbon cities or plastic-free oceans* – that do not involve socio-ecological actors as key players alongside the conventional S&T actors.

However, the convergence of these two models is unlikely to be a seamless process because–from a lagging region perspective – there has always been a deep tension between the allocation of R&I resources in EU Framework Programmes (e.g. Horizon 2020 and the proposed Horizon Europe programmes) and the R&I-based measures of Cohesion Policy (e.g. the current European Structural and Investment Funds – ESIF).

While the EC has tried to forge greater policy co-ordination between Framework Funds and Cohesion Funds, the divide has proved too difficult to bridge, mainly because the two programmes are so radically different. For example, H2020 funds are allocated on the principle of 'excellence', while ESIF funds for less developed regions are allocated on the basis of 'need'. The two programmes also operate with very different spatial coverage with H2020 funding trans-national projects, while ESIF funds national and regional projects. In short, the Framework and Cohesion programmes operate with different principles, procedures and very often with different partnerships. Coordination for and support of synergies between the two programmes 'is not optimal'.[12]

4. PLACE-BASED INNOVATION AND THE FOUNDATIONAL ECONOMY

The *foundational economy* (FE) perspective is one of the most radical concepts in the place-based policy literature because it focuses not on the fashionable sectors of the knowledge economy, but the unfashionable sectors which keep us 'safe, sound and civilised'. Foundational goods and services are purchased out of household income and/or provided free at point of use out of tax revenues.

The state is often the direct provider or funder; with the private sector increasingly delivering foundational services. The requirement for local distribution makes foundational activity immobile and much is protected from competition by the need for infrastructure investment, planning permission or government contracts.

Foundational thinking rests on two key ideas which challenge conventional assumptions about economy, society and politics:

- the well-being of citizens depends less on individual consumption and more on their social consumption of essential goods and services – from water and retail banking to schools and care homes. Individual consumption depends on market income, while foundational consumption depends on social infrastructure and delivery systems of networks and branches which are neither created nor renewed automatically, even as incomes increase;

- the distinctive, primary role of public policy should be to secure the supply of basic services for all citizens (not a quantum of economic growth and jobs). If the aim is citizen well-being, then politics at national and regional levels needs to be refocused on foundational consumption and securing universal minimum access and quality. One of the main tasks of government in this perspective, apart from helping to finance FE sectors, is to commission place-based social innovation experiments to discover what works where and why.[13]

What is the Foundational Economy?

The Foundational Economy refers to essential social goods and services that form the basis of civilized everyday life.

These include *material services* through pipes and cables, networks and branches distributing water, electricity, gas, telecoms, banking services and food; and the *providential services* of primary and secondary education, health and care for children and adults as well as income maintenance.

Foundationaleconomy.com

The FE perspective is part of a new generation of place-based conceptions primarily concerned with promoting the intrinsically significant basic needs of people, especially those who have been marginalised by the forces of globalisation, technological change and conventional policy narratives.

For example, the FE perspective resonates strongly with the *Inner Areas Strategy* developed by Fabrizio Barca and colleagues in Italy, which focuses directly on people's access to essential services, particularly health, education, and mobility.[14] It also resonates with the *Constitutional Political Economy* approach in the US, which treats housing as a gateway to an array of essential services that are deemed to be vital to human flourishing.[15] It also has much in common with the concept of *universal basic services* being championed by University College London researchers and the *everyday economy* recently proposed by the British MP Rachel Reeves.[16,17]

As with all these needs-driven models of social innovation, the FE perspective is politically challenging on three counts:

(i) it is constrained by the fact Central governments are averse to raising tax income to provide revenue support for public services like education, health and social care;
(ii) it pre-supposes governments are prepared to engage in radical re-regulation to raise the social ask on the private firms and public agencies that deliver foundational services;
(iii) it is predicated on the concept of active citizenship inasmuch as citizens are deemed to be able and willing to become co-producers of the essential services they collectively consume.

5. THE CHALLENGE OF LAGGING REGIONS: NEW DIRECTIONS IN WELSH PLACE-BASED INNOVATION POLICY

While the UK was the first country to industrialise, it was also one of the first to de-industrialise and the regions that powered the former became the hapless victims of the latter. The crisis-hit regions of inter-war Britain were the objects of the world's first regional policy, a place-based policy designed to regenerate the economically depressed industrial areas that had overly-specialised in coal, steel and heavy engineering.

Of the four depressed areas designated for economic relief by the Special Areas Act of 1934 – namely South Wales, North East England, West Cumberland and Clydeside in Scotland – only South Wales retains this sad status, with the EC classifying West Wales and the Valleys as a 'less developed region' in the current EU regional funding period (2014–2020).

This signals nothing less than a deep developmental failure in Wales as well as a devastating indictment of eighty years of British regional policy. In response, the Welsh government has begun to re-think its development strategy, which has coincided with shifts in the way lagging regions are being conceptualised.

Wales was a classic exponent of traditional regional policy, the core of which was built around two pillars: an inward investment strategy to attract foreign-owned branch plants and a state-driven strategy to build technology centres. The first pillar collapsed when the foreign plants found cheaper locations in Eastern Europe and Asia. The second pillar proved to be a costly failure because the technology centres were effectively 'cathedrals in the desert'. They were supply-side initiatives divorced from the demand-side needs of the business community.[18]

For a long time, there was little or no serious challenge to this development strategy. However, the creation of a democratically-elected National Assembly in 1999 provided institutional space for a new generation of politicians to emerge. These new politicians were more receptive to novel ideas and experimental policies, and they canvassed for a more radical *place-based* policy agenda in line with the Barca Report[19] and the new approach adopted by the World Bank (2018).[20] Today, Wales has embraced both the S&T model as well as the socio-ecological model of innovation.

Arguably, the biggest and most important change with respect to the S&T model is the new stance of the Welsh Government. As part of its S3 preparations, the Welsh Government has sought to learn the lessons of the state-centric strategy that led to the ignominious failure of its technology centres. It is now seeking to work in a more collaborative fashion through a networking approach, which is more appropriate in an era of rapid change and uncertainty.

In a series of large-scale S&T projects – such as the SPECIFIC green energy project with Swansea University and the Compound Semiconductor project with Cardiff University – the Welsh Government is learning to play roles initially envisaged by the S3 Guide, namely brokering knowledge networks between firms and universities, mobilising finance for novel projects and acting as a curator of the innovation process rather than as a central planner.[21]

However, the S&T strategy in Wales faces two major threats. First, the predicted economic effects of Brexit – with respect to export markets, foreign inward investment, cohesion policy funds, Horizon Europe funds for research and innovation and talent attraction – are overwhelmingly negative for Wales. Second, the Welsh Government has inadvertently compounded these difficulties because its education and economy departments have pursued silo-based strategies with respect to translational research and knowledge exchange. The result is Wales remains the only nation in the UK to have reduced its innovation and engagement budget to zero; a budget that financed the 'third mission' infrastructure through which universities engage with external partners in the private, public and civil sectors.[22]

The fragility of the S&T strategy stems not only from funding-related threats but also from political criticism that it was geared to a small and highly selective workforce. This criticism was especially effective from the advocates of the FE, who have sought greater recognition of the importance of basic services for citizens in a new civic politics of place.

The FE perspective maintains social well-being ought to be the primary goal of a place-based innovation policy. Well-being depends on the collective consumption of essential goods and services that are distributed to all households via networks and branches which are the infrastructure of everyday life. The two components of the FE in Wales – that is the providential services sector and the material infrastructure sector – account for almost 50% of total employment, far more than the 'next generation industries' that are the priority targets of the S&T strategy.

Box 1 Place-based policy in Wales

Well-being of Future Generations (WFG) Act 2015 (Wales)

The WFG Act introduces seven well-being goals that provide a much more capacious conception of development than the one-dimensional goal of GDP per capita growth that has hitherto dominated the public policy agenda.[23] Wales is one of the first countries to enshrine this approach in legislation that places a duty on the Welsh public sector to improve the way it achieves economic, social, environmental and cultural well-being. This is a highly distinctive initiative in the history of the place-based policy approach because it places a statutory obligation on all 44 public bodies in Wales, including the Welsh Government itself, to demonstrate how they are taking action to meet the seven national well-being goals, all of which refer to the UN's Sustainable Development Goals.

The Act also establishes a national and local framework for monitoring and delivering the well-being goals. At the national all-Wales level the Act establishes a statutory Future Generations Commissioner for Wales, whose role is to act as a guardian for the interests of future generations in Wales, and to support the public bodies listed in the Act to work towards achieving the well-being goals. At the local level the Act establishes Public Services Boards (PSBs) for each local authority area in Wales and each PSB has a duty to consult local citizens to develop a local well-being plan to improve the economic, social, environmental and cultural well-being of its area by working to achieve the well-being goals.[24]

Welsh Economic Plan 2017

The Welsh economic plan is notable for three reasons. First, it signals a new era of place-based policy by devolving more functions to the regions of Wales. Second, it introduces a new foundational economy focus by prioritizing a number of "foundation sectors", including care, food and retail, sectors that had never received any priority attention in the past. Finally, it raised the "social ask" by introducing a new and more demanding economic contract that requires businesses seeking government support to commit to fair work practices, lower carbon footprints and learning and upskilling in the work place.[25]

This emphasis on well-being resonates with new directions in the place-based policy agenda in Wales, two of which, the Wellbeing of Future Generations Act of 2015, and the Economic Action Plan (2017), are both highlighted in Box 1. Both initiatives are steps forward in that they help to create a new and more capacious conception of development, by admitting the importance of sectors, activities and workers that had fallen outside the remit of place-based innovation policy in the past.

However, the foundational perspective faces a number of problems of its own. First, foundationalists tend to be dismissive of the S&T model of innovation on the grounds it is oversold as a place-based policy for the many when its benefits are confined to the few. This binary view of place-based innovation policy is neither defensible nor necessary. Lagging regions need to embrace both the S&T and the socio-ecological models of innovation even though the former represents a small fraction of regional employment.

A second problem stems from the fact the Welsh Government presents the FE as a source of employment growth, while foundationalists see it as a means to improve the *quality* of jobs, a difference that has yet to be resolved. Thirdly, the FE model is predicated on a regulatory New Deal in which the regional state is required to re-regulate priority sectors to promote better terms and conditions and deploy its public procurement contracts – its power of purchase – in a more strategic way to the same ends.

Nevertheless, with notable exceptions, the history of public procurement in Wales is a story of untapped potential, not least because of a chronic shortage of skilled personnel in a public sector eviscerated by austerity-led public expenditure cuts. This means public purchasing is currently being driven by a narrow value-for-money focus (i.e. geared to lowest price tenders) when a *values-for-money* approach is more appropriate to the socio-ecological model that informs the foundational economy.[26] Realising the FE vision is not a soft option because it is one thing to will the ends of a fairer society and a more sustainable economy, it is another thing to have the means – the capacity and the resources – to realise those ends. Even so, the real significance of the socio-ecological model is that it opens a new debate about the meaning of place-based innovation by proposing a more capacious conception of local and regional development.

6. CHALLENGES AND POLICY RECOMMENDATIONS

Innovation policy is undergoing a period of unprecedented change as new models of innovation such as the FE perspective are challenging conventional models of innovation framed around S&T. Although these models are becoming ever more intertwined, not least because R&I policy is increasingly addressing societal challenges, this convergence is not seamless. Many lagging regions currently feel excluded from the EU's main S&T support system – the Framework Programmes for research and innovation – because the latter is allocated purely on the basis of "excellence", a principle that renders Framework Programmes a de facto regional policy for leading regions.

It is unlikely any reforms made to the S&T model will be sufficient to address the problems of lagging regions. This is why the socio-ecological model of innovation is so important in lagging regions because it has the potential to directly affect the quality of life of the many and not just the few. The FE perspective is a concrete expression of the socio-ecological model and it appeals to a wide array of citizens.

Challenge 1

In order to access R&I funds in Horizon Europe, lagging regions will need to refine their S&T capabilities because the principle of 'excellence' is likely to remain the key criterion for allocating EU resources.

Challenge 2

Cohesion Policy needs to pay far more attention to the real needs of citizens in lagging regions because, as it is presently designed and delivered, it is perceived as something that is done *to* socially-deprived communities and not *with* them, such is the lack of local ownership and community involvement.

In this regard, it is important to ensure Cohesion Policy funds can be utilised by actors and sectors of the socio-ecological model and not just the actors and sectors of the S&T model, since the former has far more resonance for the citizens of lagging regions.

Policy Recommendation 1

Breaking down the line between economic and social policy will require rethinking the objectives of policy. For example, while higher productivity is relevant to adult care provision, it cannot be the main objective of policy if care is about maintaining the social relations of older people as much as about meeting their bio-medical needs.

Policy Recommendation 2

Accept policy means learning from experiments and social innovation, which in the first instance will be local. For example, regions should experiment with policies to secure the future of grounded, family-owned SME firms and adapt training and business assistance models for micro firms (for example, through initiatives like the 'pop-up business school').

Policy Recommendation 3

Accept innovation will not abolish hard policy choices. Many sectors of the foundational economy are built on the exploitation of cheap labour; new policy objectives and instruments in sectors like tourism and care will not increase the funds available to pay wages unless consumers or taxpayers are prepared to pay more.

Policy Recommendation 4

Recognise the need to break with the political model of top–down policy with central government as the leading actor. Experimental policy will require coalitions of regional and local actors, with intermediary institutions often in the lead and central government in an enabling role.[27]

Kevin Morgan
MorganKJ@cardiff.ac.uk

REFERENCES

1 Barca F (2009) An agenda for a reformed cohesion policy: A place-based approach to meeting European Union challenges and expectations. Brussels: European Commission.

2 Moran M and Williams K (2017) Avoiding 'back to the future' policies by reforming the 'foundational economy'. In B. Jones, M. O'Donnell (eds.) *Alternatives to Neo-liberalism: Towards Equality and Democracy*, pp. 175–192. Bristol: Policy Press.

3 Rodriguez-Pose A (2018) The revenge of the places that don't matter (and what to do about it). *Cambridge Journal of Regions, Economy and Society*, 11(1), 189–209.

4 Bugge M, Coenen L, Marques P and Morgan K (2017) Governing system innovation: assisted living experiments in the UK and Norway. *European Planning Studies*, 25(12): 2138–2156.
Seyfang G and Smith A (2007) Grassroots innovations for sustainable development: towards a new research and policy agenda. *Environmental Politics*, 16(4): 584–603.

5 Foray D, Goddard J, Beldarrain XG, Landabaso M, McCann P, Morgan K, Nauwelaers C and Ortega-Argilés R (2012) Guide to Research and Innovation Strategies for Smart Specialisation (RIS3). Brussels: European Commission.
6 See page 9 in Foray et al. (2012), Reference 5.
7 See page 112–113, in Foray et al. (2012), Reference 5.
8 See page 113, in Foray et al. (2012), Reference 5.
9 Marques P and Morgan K (2018) The heroic assumptions of smart specialisation: A sympathetic critique of regional innovation policy. In A. Isaksen, R. Martin, M. Trippl (eds.) *New Avenues for Regional Innovation Systems – Theoretical Advances, Empirical Cases and Policy Lessons.* New York: Springer.
10 Foundational Economy Collective (2018) Foundational Economy. The Infrastructure of Everyday Life. Manchester: Manchester University Press.
11 European Commission (2018) EU Budget for the Future: Horizon Europe. Brussels: European Commission.
12 According to the European Commission's own internal assessment. See page 164 in European Commission (2017) In-Depth Interim Evaluation of Horizon 2020. Brussels: European Commission.
13 Foundational Economy Collective (2018), see Reference 10.
14 Barca F (2017) Inequalities, anger and the territorial dimension: The rural–urban divide, its causes and the Italian place-based strategy to tackle it. Paper presented at the Conference on Trends in inequality: social, economic and political issues. Bologna, Italy. November, 2017.
15 Rahman K. (2018) Constructing citizenship: Exclusion and inclusion through the governance of basic necessities. *Columbia Law Review,* 118(8): 2447–2503.
16 Reeves R (2018) *The Everyday Economy.* London: Labour Party.
17 Institute for Global Prosperity (2017) Social prosperity for the future: A proposal for Universal Basic Services. Institute for Global Prosperity, University College of London, London.
18 Cooke P and Morgan K (2000) *The Associational Economy: Firms, Regions and Innovation.* Oxford: Oxford University Press.
19 Barca, F. (2009), see Reference 1.
20 World Bank (2018) Rethinking Lagging Regions: Using Cohesion Policy to deliver on the potential of Europe's regions. Washington DC: World Bank.
21 Morgan K (2017) Speaking truth to power: The political dynamics of public sector innovation. In D. Kyriakou et al. (eds) *Governing Smart Specialisation,* Abingdon: Routledge.
22 Morgan K. et al. (2017) *Growing the Value of University–Business Interactions in Wales.* London: National Centre for Universities and Business.
23 Lang M and Marsden T (2018) Rethinking growth: Toward the well-being economy. A Discussion Paper. Sustainable Places Research Institute, Cardiff University.
24 Welsh Government (2016) Well-being of Futures Generations (Wales) Act, Welsh Government, Cardiff.
25 Welsh Government (2018) Economic Action Plan, Welsh Government, Cardiff.
26 Morgan K (2012) Values for Money, Agenda: The Journal of the Institute of Welsh Affairs. Cardiff: Spring.
27 Earle J, Froud J, Johalx S and Williams K (2018) Foundational economy and foundational politics. *Welsh Economic Review,* 26: 38–45. doi:http://doi.org/10.18573/wer.146

GLOSSARY

Anchor tenants. These are public organisations (e.g. research universities/public research institutes) or large private firms (e.g. multinationals) that are heavily engaged in Research and Development, and have the capacity to apply new knowledge and generate knowledge spillovers within the region in which it is located. The anchor can contribute to such effects by spinning off new companies and/or attracting new partners to the region. They are sometimes referred to as 'innovation anchors'.

Business network. A group of firms and entrepreneurs which are deliberately connected to explore, create and jointly pursue business opportunities in delivering a product/service to end-users e.g. through co-operation in a value chain value or in regional clusters.[1]

Entrepreneurial Discovery Process. An inclusive and interactive bottom–up process through which participants from different environments (policymakers, business, academia, civil society) explore and identify new domains of technological and market opportunities. Whilst these are potentially rich with numerous innovations, critically it is the interaction between participants which leads those innovations which are both attractive and feasible, to emerge.[2]

Foundational Economy. The essential goods and services which form the basis of everyday life. These include *material* services such as energy, food and water supplies, and *providential* services such as education and healthcare.

Horizontal Industrial Policy. A top–down policy framework that seeks to support the development and growth of firms across the entire economy through the provision of resources and encouragement to the economic environment more generally, which make it easier for businesses and individuals to be productive. Examples include generic skills and education programmes, infrastructure and generic tax incentives to promote entrepreneurship, investment and Research and Development (R&D).

Industrial Strategy. A broad framework of policies, which serve to stimulate and support the direction of future industrial growth.[3] These may include support for 'infant industry', trade and FDI policies, science and technology policies, state procurement, regulation, anti-trust and merger policy, intellectual property rights, and the development of regional clusters and regions.

https://doi.org/10.1080/2578711X.2019.1621104

Industry 4.0 (I4.0). This refers to the recent trend of automation, digitalisation and data exchange in manufacturing technologies. It includes cyber-physical systems, the Internet of things, cloud computing and cognitive computing.

Knowledge networks. Describes interconnected economic actors sharing knowledge and potentially collaborating to deliver innovative solutions to complex technical problems.

Place-based Industrial Strategy. A bottom up perspective that builds a framework for local economic growth and development. It strongly recognises that it is the interaction of participants (policy-makers, business, academia, civil society) and local institutions within a particular geographic space, that can best identify and implement those policies, suited to their own circumstances.

Regional Innovation Ecosystem. This describes how firms and other actors, within a geographic, territorial domain, interact to stimulate entrepreneurial endeavours that lead to innovative and innovation-based outcomes.

Research and Innovation Strategies for Smart Specialisation (RIS3). This describes the European Union's (EU) 2020 Innovation programme which invokes the key elements of S3.

Smart Specialisation Strategy (S3). A place-based approach to innovation-based (broadly defined), economic development and growth. Existing and potential strengths of a sub-national level of geography, ripe for strategic public policy intervention are identified through an Entrepreneurial Discovery Process with wide stakeholder involvement.

Triple Helix Model. Describes the roles, responsibilities and interactions between three actors (university, industry and government) within a general framework for exploring complex innovation dynamics and for informing national, regional and international innovation and development policy-making[4].

Vertical Industrial Policy. A top–down and selective policy framework which seeks to support the development and growth of specific firms, sectors/industries or particular clusters.

References

1 Österle H, Fleisch E and Rainer A (2001) *Business Networking: Shaping Collaboration between Enterprises*. Berlin: Springer-Verlag.

2 See http://s3platform.jrc.ec.europa.eu/entrepreneurial-discovery-edp [Accessed 26 October 2018].

3 See http://researchbriefings.files.parliament.uk/documents/CBP-7682/CBP-7682.pdf [Accessed 26 October 2018].

4 See https://triplehelix.stanford.edu/3helix_concept [Accessed 26 October 2018].

For Product Safety Concerns and Information please contact our EU representative GPSR@taylorandfrancis.com Taylor & Francis Verlag GmbH, Kaufingerstraße 24, 80331 München, Germany

Batch number: 10726540

Printed by Printforce, the Netherlands